GR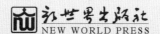WING
WITH
CHINA
MNC EXECUTIVES TALK
ABOUT CHINA

Compiled by Zhu Ling

新世界出版社
NEW WORLD PRESS

First Edition 2009
Compiled by Zhu Ling
Edited by Li Shujuan and Ge Wencong
Cover Design by Li Hong

ISBN 978-7-80228-992-5

Published by
  NEW WORLD PRESS
  24 Baiwanzhuang Street, Beijing 100037, China

Distributed by
  NEW WORLD PRESS
  24 Baiwanzhuang Street, Beijing 100037, China
  Tel: 86-10-68995968
  Fax: 86-10-68998705
  Website: www.newworld-press.com
  E-mail: frank@nwp.com.cn

Printed in the People's Republic of China

PREFACE

It is often said that each and every foreign enterprise in China has made a contribution in one way or another to the success of the country's economic reforms in the past 30 years.

They have, indeed, all played a key role in driving the rapid pace of industrialization, which has brought unprecedented prosperity in its wake. Vastly improved living standards have created a strong demand for goods and services, which, in turn, has brought unmatched opportunities for many multinational companies to make sound profits, part of which has undoubtedly been reinvested in research and development for better products and services.

This has produced many star performers in their respective industries and international organizations. Each of these companies has a fascinating tale to tell, and some of them were generous enough to share their experience with readers of *China Daily*. The adventures of these corporate pioneers in China, as told by their CEOs, were documented in a series that ran in *Business Weekly*, published by and distributed with *China Daily* every Monday.

The list includes companies in different industries and service sectors. Some came to manufacture, either on their own or in joint ventures with domestic enterprises. Others came to sell their products, and, in some cases, helped create markets that did not exist before. Moreover, there were those who came to render special services, and, in the process, helped promote the standard of such services in China.

Since the beginning of economic reforms, China has welcomed investors and traders from other economies, regions and countries on the principle of mutual benefit.

The rapid industrialization of the Pearl River Delta (PRD) Region in Guangdong Province, initially driven mainly by the capital from Hong Kong manufacturers and exporters, is a case in point. It created the platform that eventually made PRD a world-famous industrial powerhouse, and, in the process, generated sufficient wealth to facilitate Hong Kong's smooth transformation into a high-value-added financial and service center.

The modern automobile industry in China can be said to have been built on the investment and expertise of foreign carmakers in joint ventures with their respective domestic partners. Most major car makers from the US, Europe and Japan have benefited from the explosive growth of the domestic market.

Their Chinese partners, meanwhile, have gained financial resources and secured the technological know-how to develop own-brand models for the domestic market. Some domestic carmakers are now aggressively exploring opportunities of exporting to the United States and Europe.

Foreign companies have also played a key role in the development of China's services sector. Nearly all major international hotel chains own and/or operate properties in various cities on the mainland. Four major international accounting firms have contributed directly and indirectly to the rise of the standard of corporate governance, enabling many mainland enterprises to tap the resources of the world's major capital markets.

Some mainland cities, including Shanghai, Guangzhou and Shenzhen, are playing host to the world's foremost logistics companies. The world's major banks, with their head offices in Shanghai, are rapidly expanding their lending, deposit and trade financing businesses not only in the coastal regions but also in the industrial heartlands in the central and western parts of the country.

The distribution and retail sector has also benefited from the foreign hypermarket chains that have helped fundamentally change the shopping habits of millions of Chinese consumers in cities.

As an active participant in the epic economic reform that China has shepherded, every one of these multinational companies has a fascinating story to tell.

Among the companies featured in the series are Airbus, Siemens, BASF and Mercedes-Benz from Europe, GE and HP from the US, Toshiba and Fujifilm from Japan, and Nokia from Finland.

For a more general view of the foreign business communities in China, we have interviewed the heads of AmCham-China and South Korea Chamber of Commerce.

These articles in *Business Weekly* series are compiled in this book as a fitting commemoration of the 30th anniversary of economic reform and opening-up, which has brought the world to China and aligned its corporate and consumption trends with that in the rest of the world.

We are sure they will be as useful and entertaining for you to read as they were exciting and satisfying for us to produce.

Zhu Ling
Editor-in-chief of China Daily
October 26, 2008

CONTENTS

3M
AHEAD OF THE CURVE *1*

ACCA
TOTAL ACCOUNTABILITY *11*

adidas
IN SHAPE *19*

AIRBUS
SOARING SALES *31*

AmCham-China
AMCHAMP *43*

BASF
GOOD CHEMISTRY *49*

Carrefour
FRENCH CONNECTION *55*

CATERPILLAR
DIGGING IN *63*

CISCO
REACHING OUT *71*

Deloitte Touche Tohmatsu
NUMBER CRUNCHING *77*

EU
THRIVING PARTNERSHIP *85*

FUJIFILM
CHINA FOCUS 91

GE
RISING TOGETHER 101

GOODYEAR
SILENT RUNNING 107

HILL & KNOWLTON
BUILDING RELATIONS 117

HP
BREAKING GROUND 123

InBev
BREWING PROFITS 137

Marriott
ROOM WITH A VIEW 147

McDonald's
MC GROWING 161

Mercedes-Benz
BIG BENZ 167

MICHELIN
GREEN WHEELS 179

NOKIA
NOKIA RECHARGES 189

P&G
MASS APPEAL 201

ROHM AND HAAS
THE RIGHT PLACE 211

Schneider Electric
PLUGGED IN 217

Shell
MEETING IN THE MIDDLE 229

Siemens
POWERING CHINA 237

South Korea Chamber of Commerce
GROWING TOGETHER 245

TOSHIBA
GROWING WITH CHINA 251

Volkswagen
IN EARLY, ON TOP 263

The World Bank
INVESTMENT RETURNS 277

AHEAD OF THE CURVE

After 15 years at the helm of 3M's operation in China, Kenneth Yu's favorite pastime after work is walking along the Shanghai Bund and looking at the old Shanghai Mansion.

Twenty-four years ago, in a small office on the 14th floor of the Shanghai Mansion, 3M's China Corporation was officially established. Yu clearly recalls those days when it was just a small group with seven employees, and only involved in trading.

"It was only six years after China started its reform and opening-up experiment in 1978," managing director of 3M China tells *China Business Weekly* in a recent interview in his Shanghai office.

"That was in our early phase. Many people were uncertain whether it would be successful. So we were just trying and waiting for business opportunities."

Yu adds that the lack of a professional local leader stalled the company's market exploration work in China at that time.

But the small 3M China still holds special significance for both the company and Shanghai municipality.

It was the first wholly foreign-funded enterprise registered in Shanghai. Since then, the city has grown into a major economic hub famous for the large number of China headquarters of foreign companies. And 3M China has grown into the third largest overseas subsidiary of the US-based diversified technology company with 5,000 employees.

Over the past 24 years, the company has invested over US$600 million in China, establishing 12 branches, eight manufacturing bases, 22 regional offices, three technical centers and one R&D center in different regions of China. It has also developed from the single trading business to seven large manufacturing teams covering the chemical industry, electronics industry, telecommunications, medical treatment, traffic and consumer markets.

3M's Shanghai office

"We had far more success than we had expected. 3M China is expected to be the biggest overseas subsidiary outside the US in the coming years. Over the past decade, the company has grown at an annual rate of over 20 to 30 percent on average," Yu says.

Yu emphasizes that the turning point came in 1993. At that time, 3M bet much on Yu, appointing him as the head of 3M China in the hope that his experience in the local market could boost its China sales.

The first thing Yu did was to travel to China's main cities to explore the different market demands.

"What inspired me most was the difficulty of telecommunications," Yu says. "Without open telecommunications it was impossible to achieve the goal of economic reform and opening-up."

3M engineer works in a lab.

In addition, he learned that the cost of installing a phone was more than 4,000 *yuan* at that time (when the average salary for urban workers was around 300 to 400 *yuan*).

So Yu made one of the brightest decisions — investing in China's telecommunications industry in late 1993.

3M engineer works in a lab.

"Advanced technology could help boost the output of the telecommunication facilities, which could reduce installation costs and make phones affordable for residents' homes," Yu explains.

The action, which came ahead of all the domestic manufacturers in the telecommunications industry, generated great success for 3M China, and also accelerated the speed of China's new era. And under Yu's leadership, after five years 3M China had more than US$100 million in sales revenue in 1998.

Next Yu thought that highway construction might be the country's next major development goal, so 3M invested in manufacturing traffic and road signs.

The auto, electronics, and household appliance industries were next. Step by step, 3M has been expanding its business supplying more than 60,000 products to China as well as developing advanced technologies.

"3M China has been growing together with the Chinese

economy. By operating in China for over 24 years, I have witnessed its fast development, especially since the 1990s," Yu says.

However, 3M's success lies more in the ability to forecast various market trends, Yu points out. "A key value of 3M is meeting our customers' needs. And we have to exceed their expectations." 3M China has also realized that its business success would be better by concentrating on serving the Chinese market, he says.

The 1990s also brought more competitors to China, Yu says, so 3M braved the challenge in 1994 by establishing its first technical service center in Beijing to teach customers how to use 3M's various products and use their inputs for further research and product development.

"We are working here, exploring the domestic business opportunities and providing products to meet the local market demands," Yu adds.

In 2007, the company invested US$40 million to establish a research and development (R&D) center in Caohejing New Technology Park in Shanghai. It's 3M's fourth largest R&D center and all the researchers in the Shanghai R&D center are Chinese.

"It manifests the fact that China has become 3M's most significant market and the company hopes to keep pace with the country's booming economy and support the country's development goals," says an engineer in the R&D center.

With China's recent move to make energy conservation and pollution control top priorities on the national agenda, Yu is proud that 3M China was the first company to install energy-saving thermal oxidation furnaces in 1993. "Energy saving is one of 3M's core requirements worldwide, so we have to do it in China."

The manager admits that there is one green opportunity 3M hasn't explored, and he says that will change.

"As a leading diversified technology provider, 3M has the advanced technology to better protect the environment. We need to do a better job of sharing our expertise and experience with local companies, working in partnership to help achieve China's energy savings and emission control goals," Yu says. "I will make an effort to do this in the coming years."

3Memory Lane

Kenneth Yu has worked in 3M for almost 40 years. After working in 3M Hong Kong and Singapore for 24 years, Yu brought the company's operation to China where he has headed 3M China's growth for the last 15 years.

From a small office with only seven employees, to a huge team with 5,000 workers, eight manufacturing plants and a top R&D center, 3M China has become the company's branch with the most potential and 30 to 35 percent annual sales growth in recent years.

During a recent interview in Yu's Shanghai office with *China Business Weekly* reporter, Yu shared his experi-

Kenneth Yu,
Managing director of 3M
China

ences with 3M China since 1993 as well as his view on China's economic reform and rapid growth.

Q: 3M is famous for its diversified technologies and products. In China, you lead seven large teams that provide more than 60,000 products for the local market. How do you lead such a huge team and keep an annual sales growth rate of 30 to 35 percent?

A: It is hard but it is interesting for me. We create new products almost every day. We watch the changing market to adjust our business focus. Every day is new and innovative for us.

Innovation is the most important direction for my operation and it makes us grow. In 2007, 3M China contributed more than 20 billion *yuan* for sales, which accounted for around 10 percent of the company's global revenue.

But I think there are still huge opportunities for us to make further growth. That is why we have been continuing to add to our investments here, the market with the most potential in the world. And perhaps the annual growth rate of 30 to 35 percent won't satisfy me in the coming years.

Q: What is the core value of your leadership in 3M China?

A: People, for sure. Take me as an example. From 1969, when I was 19, I came to 3M Hong Kong. So far, I have worked in 3M for nearly 40 years. But I am not an exception. In 3M China, all the people at the middle and high leadership levels have an average of 17 years working at 3M. I think a company should make an effort to preserve its talents. It is the key value for our operation.

If a team of workers has worked for many years, they will have a perfect tacit understanding. It is easy to shape common consciousness.

3M grants several large awards annually to encourage innovation. In 3M, we trust everyone. We encourage everyone and have enough room for free creation and thinking. That is why we've had so many innovations in recent years.

Q: **During your 15 years of heading 3M China, have you encountered any challenges?**

A: So far, I still feel a little disappointed that I ignored spreading our brand from the start. As the first multinational company registered and established in Shanghai, 3M is still not well-known to most Chinese people.

When you mention "3M" in China, people may think the brand is only a Post-it note producer. So, that's 3M's most famous product here. Indeed, it is the smallest department. That is my fault, I only engaged in spreading the brand to business partners and ignored the huge number of Chinese consumers. Fortunately, I have woken up to this problem now and I am trying my best to improve it.

Q: **What is your view on China's 30 years of reform and opening-up?**

A: I think China has made great changes since 1978. About 25 years ago, I took a business tour to Shanghai from Hong Kong. At that time, it was difficult for me to find a hotel. But today, you can see so many five-star hotels located in the city, as well as top level airports and tele-communication facilities.

As a 40-year "veteran" in the company, I think I was fortunate to witness some of the company's dramatic shifts in China's market — from a small office that only had seven employees, to one of the most significant groups for 3M in the global market, with a team of more than 5,000 people, 22 offices and eight manufacturing plants in different regions of China.

It is the best stage for all the companies to invest and grow. But I think it poses more challenges to us. The country is still going in a good direction. Its excellent growth surprises us every day, and being here we have to be innovative every day.

By BAO WANXIAN

ACCA

TOTAL ACCOUNTABILITY

Many people may say an accountant works simply by adding and subtracting figures. But is it really as simple as it looks?

For those with at least some knowledge of China's past three decades of economic reforms, the answer is definitely "No".

China's successful transition from a rigid, centrally planned economy to a market-oriented one has been accurately summed up as a process of "reform and opening-up". But such a generalization may ignore some basic and crucial, but less obvious elements of the economy, such as accounting.

An inherent part of opening-up is more engagement with international investors and traders and the parties involved need to find a common language that is known to them all. English is the obvious choice and that's why China has become the country with the largest number of English learners. But foreign investors and traders may need more than a common language. "International investors were unable to understand Chinese companies' financial sheets in the planned economy period," says Liu Yuting, head of the accounting section of the Ministry of Finance.

China had adopted accounting standards which originated in the former Soviet Union but were tailored to China's economic realities. They were different from the general principles Western accountants abided by. Cross-border communication and business, therefore, became difficult not only because of political barriers, but because enterprises across the border spoke different "corporate languages".

From the early 1980s, right after China started its reform and opening-up drive, Chinese accounting researchers had begun to introduce Western accounting standards and China established formal corporate accounting standards in 1992.

The establishment of the country's stock market in the early 1990s made it more necessary for the accounting standards to be updated and accepted by all enterprises.

In December 1993, the National People's Congress passed the revised "CPA Law", which came into effect in 1994. It mandated that China adopt a completely new accounting system and ended the old planned economy accounting practice.

Richard Aitken Davies,
President of ACCA

Standard accounting rules would promote the long-term sustainable growth of enterprises, help standardize capital market rules and facilitate auditing, thus becoming part of the financial infrastructure that "underpins and drives China's extraordinary economic success," says Richard Aitken Davies, president of the UK-based Association of Chartered Certified Accountants (ACCA).

Since 2002, Liu and his team at the Ministry of Finance have been endeavoring to further update China's accountancy standards to get them in line with the international ones.

On the other front, international accounting bodies have entered China to help it get in line with globally accepted accounting principles and to train professionals, with the ACCA playing a leading role.

ACCA, the largest and fastest-growing global professional accountancy body in the world, with over 320,000 members and students in 170 countries, entered the mainland in 1988, 10 years after China started its opening-up drive.

ACCA and China Institute of Certified Public Accountants (CICPA) organised the third Training for Trainers program to promote international accounting standards in China in 2008.

Allen Blewitt, former chief executive of ACCA, who passed the mantle to Helen Brand in September 2008, had come to China even earlier and his impressions were fresh and unique.

Helen Brand,
Chief executive, ACCA

Blewitt first visited China in 1977 when the country had just emerged from the "cultural revolution" (1966-1976) and was looking for a path that could bring the nation out of chaos and towards economic prosperity.

To his surprise, he found ordinary Chinese showed an unbending spirit, which later proved to be the underpinning element for China's rise as a global economic powerhouse.

"It was (in a people's commune) in Hunan that I met a number of young Chinese students at a sports stadium, where primary school children were being assessed for their athletic abilities," says Blewitt, who was then on a study tour of young Australians. At that time, athletics were not as common as today.

He asked their teacher why they could be so concentrated on athletics and the teacher said, "One day, China will be readmitted to the Olympic movement".

The philosophical sports teacher was right. Thirty-one years later, Beijing successfully hosted the Olympic Games.

Hungry for Accountants

"The indelible memory of the 1977 visit remains; everywhere we went Chinese citizens were working steadily and unceasingly in factories, schools and in the communes," he says. "There was a great faith that China was emerging."

In the coming years, Deng Xiaoping led the country to liberalize the rural economy by allowing farmers to work on their own instead of on the communes, and generally unleashing the "entrepreneurial spirit of the Chinese people". "It was a small step, but it was followed by big steps of liberalizing economy shortly afterwards," Blewitt says.

It is not clear whether Blewitt's unique China experience motivated him in his ACCA years to ultimately influence the ACCA management to enter China. But certainly the association, as foresighted as the Chinese teacher Blewitt had met, had foreseen China's economic potential and entered the country to gain an early advantage.

A group of trainers take a photo with their teachers during an ACCA-CICPA training program.

"We were aware from our experience elsewhere in the world how important professional accountants might be to the success of economies," says Davies. "So we felt it was an opportune time for us to come and see what we could contribute to the Chinese market." Its contribution is huge.

"The rapidly growing economy in China needs armies of high-quality accountants, and we at ACCA have done a great job in this regard and are cooperating with many local partners to meet such needs to fuel economic growth by training and nurturing more high-caliber professionals," says Kelly Chan, financial controller of Moet Hennessy Diageo Hong Kong Ltd. and ACCA Hong Kong president.

ACCA has gone from a first batch of 30 students in Beijing to 20,000 members and 32,000 students, with 27 exam centers, 600 approved employers and four offices in Beijing, Shanghai, Guangzhou and Hong Kong. Many of its students have become backbones of the industry and their employers.

"In the past two decades, ACCA has helped China train a good number of professionals versed in international accounting standards and practices, who have played a conducive role in China's transformation to a market economy," says Tang Yunwei, partner of Ernst & Young and the first ACCA honorary member from China.

"I hope ACCA will continue to contribute to China's economic growth by doing the same good job as it has done in the past two decades."

For many who attend ACCA tests, the exams are in a sense as important as the national college entrance exams, because they may both change the fate of the youth.

"ACCA was the biggest turning point in my life," says Dai Xibao, deputy general manager of Internal Audit Department of Aluminum Corporation of China Limited.

Dai was not in financial or accounting major during his university years. "ACCA provided me with a high-level platform to embark on my financial career," says Dai, who initially graduated from the Department of Philosophy at Peking University and used to be a college teacher.

The organization has attributed its success in China to the country's rising economic prowess, which creates increasing demand for high-caliber accounting professionals. "China has contributed so much to ACCA's reputation and influence over such a short period of time," says Helen Brand, ACCA chief executive.

For China, however, the benefits are mutual and the organization's vision is behind its success.

"By entering China, you've chosen the right place (to expand your business) and that's because you have thorough knowledge of China," says Wang Jun, Vice-minister of Finance.

By XIN ZHIMING

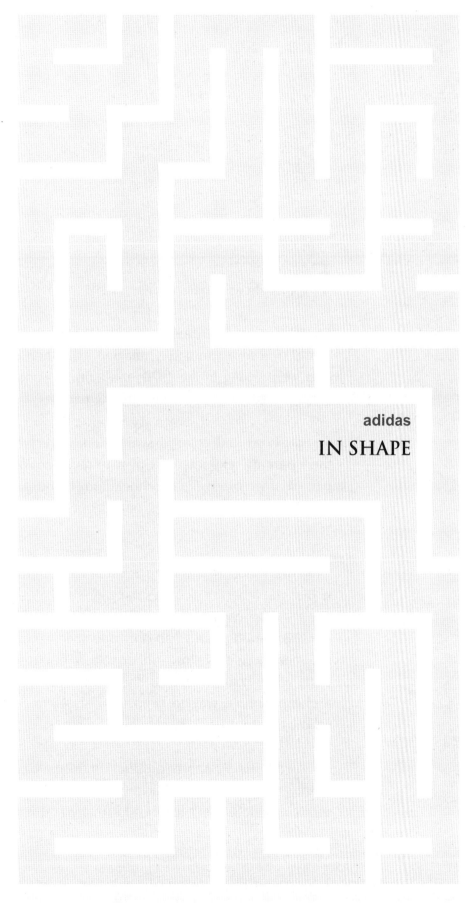

adidas
IN SHAPE

For young Chinese urbanites, owning several pairs of sports shoes is natural.

Sports apparel is an indispensable part of their fashion sense. And they can hardly imagine that when their parents were young in the 1970s the ultimate sports dream was perhaps just a pair of ping-pong paddles.

Sports shoes and colorful sweat suits were far beyond their parents' expectations at a time when wearing a pair of army green *Jiefang* (liberation) brand shoes was enough to make the wearer stand out from his or her "comrades".

Until the 1980s, when living became easier, sports slowly became a part of people's daily lives.

However, sports shoes had only one style — white canvas sneakers with yellow rubber soles. People still recall using white chalk to "paint" the shoes after washing — a cheap, simple way to keep their shoes from turning yellow due to the low quality laundry soaps.

Although China's sports products industry has a short history, it has developed at an amazing speed. Today, sports products aren't luxuries for many and it's difficult to spot identical shoes being worn on the streets. According to statistics from World Federation of Sporting Goods Industry, China now accounts for more than 65 percent of sports goods production in the world.

Nearly all the international sports brands have entered China to further mine the market potential. They are not only the creators but also the beneficiaries from China's speedy development.

For the German sports conglomerate adidas, China has become the most important market and is expected to be its second-largest revenue market after the US by the end of 2008.

An athlete wears adidas wrestling playsuit at the Olympic cradle land in Greece. Since 1928 Amsterdam Olympics, adidas has always been a partner with Olympics.

"The adidas Group has been active in the Chinese market for over two decades, and during that time we have borne witness to the remarkable changes that have transformed the country, changes that the adidas Group too has directly experienced and is honored to have been a part of," says Wolfgang Bentheimer, managing director of adidas China.

Since his first visit to China in 1998 and after traveling to the country many times in the following years, Bentheimer says, "I could see and experience first-hand the fast development and progress the country has made. It is incredible to see how the Chinese consumer market has evolved in only a few years, and what potential this market still bears for brands and those companies which are able to meet the needs and desires of Chinese consumers."

In the first half of 2008, adidas Group's sales in China increased over 60 percent on a currency-neutral basis.

Just one day before the opening of Beijing 2008 Olympic Games this August, adidas announced that in terms of market share, it was the leading sports brand in China for the first time, where nearly 50 percent of all its products are being produced.

Ethiopian long-distance running legend Haile Gebrselassie cheered after winning in 10,000-m race at 1996 Atlanta Olympics, wearing adidas sportswear.

"The Beijing 2008 Olympic Games served as a platform for us to reach market leadership with our brand adidas in the Chinese market. Our design and development center in Shanghai will keep creating products that inspire consumers around Asia and other parts of the world. We clearly expect our success story in China to continue," says Bentheimer.

"The adidas Group has excelled in the first half of 2008, achieving double-digit top-

and bottom-line growth. Our business in China was a big contributor to this growth," says Herbert Hainer, CEO and chairman of adidas AG.

Adidas' role as the official sportswear partner of the Beijing 2008 Olympic Games, the expansion of distribution for adidas and Reebok, as well as the development of TaylorMade-adidas Golf have been the primary growth drivers for the company in China.

"We are well on track to reach our sales target of more than one billion euros for the adidas Group in China by 2010," says Hainer.

Herbert Hainer, CEO and chairman of adidas AG, raising the Olympic flame as torchbearer in Beijing hours before the 2008 Olympics opening ceremony.

Grow with China

"Adidas has a long history of involvement in sports in China. Adidas' first cooperation with Chinese soccer dates back to 1981 and continues to the present day," says Bentheimer.

Adidas has also been heavily involved with the development of basketball in China, too. The first contract with the China Basketball Association was signed in 1985. Adidas has sponsored different professional basketball teams in China over the past few years.

Adidas started business in China in the early 1990s and founded a subsidiary in 1997. Back then, adidas China only had around 20 employees. But now it has more than 1,300 employees with offices in Shanghai, Beijing and Guangzhou. At the end of 2007, the adidas Group operated 4,800 stores in China and is planning to take that number to 5,900 in 2008.

By the end of 2010, the German brand expects to have more than 7,000 adidas and Reebok stores all across China.

"Sport has enjoyed a growing popularity among Chinese over the past decades. More and more people are living an active life, participating in such sports as basketball, football, badminton and running," says Bentheimer.

"With the fast growth of the Chinese economy over the last years, Chinese consumers have enjoyed growing disposable incomes that they are willing to spend on luxury products and international labels including sporting goods," he adds.

In July 2008, adidas opened its largest store in the world — the four-floor adidas Brand Center in Beijing, with a size of 3,170 sq. m.

"Now adidas is entering sixth-tier cites in China. We are really distributing across China," says Bentheimer.

He says that at present, 60 percent of the sports brand's revenue is contributed by the first-tier to third-tier cities, while the rest 40 percent comes from the fourth-tier to sixth-tier cities.

Straight Talk

Wolfgang Bentheimer is the managing director of adidas China. Since he began his career with the company in the late 1990s, Wolfgang has taken adidas to new heights across several markets. This includes maintaining adidas China as one of the best performing subsidiaries in the adidas Group.

Growing with China in early times and sponsoring Beijing 2008 Olympic Games, adidas has been deeply rooted in the Chinese market and aims to further develop in this fastest shaping market.

Sportswear displayed in adidas' first Brand Center in downtown Beijing. The four-floor store, opened in July 2008, is the company's biggest of its kind worldwide.

In an exclusive interview with *China Business Weekly* reporter, Bentheimer shares his opinions on his company's development and China's economic reform and rapid growth.

Wolfgang Bentheimer,
Managing director of
adidas China

Q: What's the biggest challenge for your company in the Chinese market?

A: In the Chinese market, the "war for talents" is probably among the toughest worldwide. For us, getting the right people for our organization in order to support our fast growth is a key challenge.

However, our involvement as official sportswear partner of the recent Beijing 2008 Olympic Games as well as other marketing activities we are rolling out nationwide will help us to further strengthen our branding in the eyes of external talents.

For our current employees, adidas Group China is running staff engagement programs in order to engage and motivate our employees. During the Beijing 2008 Olympic Games, we brought all of our China-based staff to Beijing so that everybody working for the adidas Group in China got to experience the Olympic Games firsthand and truly felt as a part of this sponsorship.

Another challenge for our group in China is to expand and optimize the distribution network fast enough, in order to make our brands available and accessible to the relevant brand consumer all over China. Therefore we need to continuously focus our energy on further expansions.

Increased competition from sport brands as well as from leisure and casual brands presents another challenge in the Chinese market, since the growth and size of this market make it increasingly attractive to new players.

However, adidas has an excellent position as a premium brand in the sports and sports lifestyle sectors in China and we will continue to put emphasis on further innovations, new products and exciting marketing campaigns to lead in this important market.

Consumers can design and tailor their own sports shoes in adidas stores in Beijing and get them delivered within 25-30 days.

Q: In your view, what are the key elements driving your success in China?

A: The biggest success driver in our development here in the Chinese market has been to very closely connect with our consumers, to offer innovative products, to launch meaningful communication concepts and to create retail environments in which consumers can experience our brands at their very best.

At the adidas Group, we have a first class team in place around the globe with extensive experience, and we have used this experience to become one of the leaders in the sporting goods industry. Here in China, our team consists of very strong members with vast local and international experience, making sure that consumer needs are put first and that local executions of global concepts are adapted to local needs.

The recent adidas China Olympic Campaign is a great example of our local team taking over the initiative and coming up with a campaign specially tailored for the Chinese market. It is the biggest campaign that adidas ever rolled out in a single market and it was developed by our Chinese marketing team.

Q: What's your view of China's sports market after the Olympics? Will there be more competitions, challenges, or opportunities?

A: The importance of sports and the sporting goods industry will further increase in China. The adidas Group believes that the Olympic Games will support this development. Also, growing income will make sporting goods affordable for a bigger number of Chinese consumers.

For the adidas Group, China will continue to be an important manufacturing and sales market with nearly 50 percent of all our products being produced in China.

Q: As president of a multinational company's branch in China, what's your view on China's 30 years of reform and opening-up?

A: These past 30 years have seen some of the most incredible social and economic changes in history, as China has grown at an astonishing pace to become — in just a few years — a major world power, a truly influential player on the global stage. This status was confirmed by the fantastic success of the Beijing 2008 Olympic Games, which offered the world an opportunity to experience and better understand this new, confident China. And as the official sportswear partner of the Games the adidas brand was proud to be working alongside the people of China to make these Games successful.

Over the last 30 years, we have seen incredible economic growth in China, growth that has transformed the country since the reform and opening-up policy was launched.

Indeed, China is now seen as being one of the key strategic markets in the global economy. With that, the lives of people across the country have been transformed. Hundreds of millions have been lifted out of poverty, perhaps the most impressive victory in the battle against poverty that we have ever seen. People now enjoy a better standard of life and they have more choices available to them than ever before.

As these changes have been felt across the nation over the last few decades, the adidas Group too has grown together with the Chinese market. China is now one of our most important markets globally, and we are experiencing sustained growth here, led by the adidas brand's association with the Beijing 2008 Olympic Games.

This is a historic time for the adidas Group and for China. While we look back over the successes of recent years we also look forward to decades of continued growth and prosperity for China.

By LI FANGFANG

AIRBUS

SOARING SALES

Laurence Barron,
President of Airbus
China

Making a smooth transition into a new job in a foreign country is a challenge for anyone, especially for those who have little work or travel experience in their new homes.

But not Airbus China president Laurence Barron when he moved from Airbus headquarters in France in January 2004 to lead the company's operation in China.

"I found the transition relatively easy. Things have turned out far busier and far more exciting than what I had anticipated," says Barron, adding that he was too busy to contemplate on the transition.

When Barron came to China, Airbus aircraft only accounted for 23 percent of the Chinese fleet in service. But by the end of 2007, the figure had shot up to 37 percent. China is also increasingly integrated into Airbus' industrial production, from supplying components to hosting the company's first aircraft final assembly line outside Europe.

"I didn't expect the sales volumes. Nobody ever dreamed that we would build a final assembly line anywhere outside Europe," Barron says. "We had a lot more success than we had expected."

Airbus' success story in China reflects how the country's aviation industry has taken flight.

Since 1978, the country's air traffic has maintained an annual growth rate of 18 percent, almost double of China's average GDP growth rate and three times the world's average growth rate of air transportation during the same period, according to figures from the Civil Aviation Administration of China (CAAC), the nation's industry watchdog.

China will remain the world's largest commercial aircraft market outside the United States for the next 20 years, according to estimates by the US aircraft manufacturer Boeing. It forecasts China will need about 3,400 new airplanes, worth US$340 billion, over the next two decades, and the country's fleet will nearly quadruple to

The world's largest commercial airplane Airbus A380 flew to Beijing for a technical route proving in China in November 2006.

Airbus' first aircraft
final assembly line
(FAL) outside Europe
— A320 FAL in Tianjin.

4,460 by 2026. Airbus has similar forecasts that China, driven by a double-digit economic growth rate, will need 100 to 150 aircraft per year for the next 20 years.

Making Its Mark

Airbus sold its first plane to China in 1985, when Boeing had a 13-year head start. The aircraft, an A310, was delivered to the Shanghai branch of the CAAC, which later became China Eastern Airlines. Airbus China Co. Ltd. was established in 1994.

With only a seven percent market share in China in 1995, the European company was unknown to most Chinese people. Some thought it was an airport shuttle bus company, while others said it was a bus producer. Few linked its name to aircraft manufacturing.

But the European company was committed to long-term development in China.

The Chinese airline industry transported 185 million passengers in 2007, up 15.9 percent year on year. The Chinese airlines only carried 3.43 million passengers in 1980. China only had 140 airplanes in 1980, but it now has a fleet of over 1,000 planes.

China is expected to replace France as the world's top tourism destination by 2014 and it has already overtaken Japan to become Asia's largest source of outbound travelers. The flourishing economy also makes the country one of the top draws in global business travel market.

The civil aviation industry also went through a series of reforms that included allowing private investors to set up airlines, simplifying procedures for approving new air routes, and allowing foreign investment in airlines and airports. China also opened its skies wider to foreign airlines and signed bilateral aviation agreements with 106 countries by the end of 2006, according to the CAAC.

"Our growth was certainly not possible without the reform and opening-up of the market here," Barron says.

Commitment to Customers

Besides providing the right products for the market, Barron says timely and efficient customer support and service have also helped Airbus achieve fast growth in China.

The Toulouse, France-based company set up an aviation training and support joint venture in 1996 with China Aviation Supplies Import and Export Group Corp. The center, a 50-50 joint venture, is located near the Beijing Capital

International Airport. It was the first of its kind built by a foreign aircraft manufacturer in China that combined simulator training for airlines and customer support facilities.

The customer services department provides on-site technical support for airline operations in 20 Chinese cities.

Airbus has a network of spare parts and support centers in Beijing, Frankfurt, Hamburg, Singapore and Washington, D.C. It has a spare parts warehouse worth more than US$30 million in Beijing and contracted another one in Shanghai in 2006.

The Airbus customer support center in Beijing is working toward a regional hub that serves the whole Asian market. Some of the Chinese engineers have been traveling to serve regional customers in Myanmar, Vietnam, Siberia, Indonesia and Cambodia.

While fighting head-to-head with Boeing on "traditional battlefields" — China's three largest airline groups — Airbus is also expanding in an emerging market: start-up private air carriers.

"Our strategy is to establish stable relationships with all our customers, from the biggest to the smallest, from major airlines to regional airlines and start-ups," Barron says. Currently four out of the seven private carriers in China are flying Airbus A320 family aircraft.

"These start-up airlines all have ambitious plans to expand their fleet. Nobody would neglect this market," says Liu Weimin, director of the Aviation Laws Research Center at the Civil Aviation Management Institute of China.

The world's largest commercial airplane Airbus A380 flew to Beijing for a technical route proving in China in November 2006.

Engineers work in an
Airbus aircraft.

A major reason for Airbus' success with Chinese private airlines, Barron says, is its close partnership with international leasing companies such as GE Commercial Aviation Services and International Lease Finance Corp. The four Chinese private airlines started their businesses by leasing Airbus aircraft.

Due to strong market demand, the new aircraft manufactured by both Boeing and Airbus have basically been on order for the next five years so that it is difficult for them to meet short-term needs. But for start-up companies, the primary question is how to purchase new aircraft as soon as possible for business operation.

However, since one-third of Airbus A320 family aircraft have been sold to international leasing companies, it might be a way for the start-up companies to have aircraft available much sooner by cooperating with those leasing firms, says Barron, who has specialized in aircraft financing at Airbus for more than 10 years.

A Ride Together

Airbus swept the Chinese media in 2007 for two historic events: a one-week tour of China by the world's largest airliner A380 and a groundbreaking ceremony in Tianjin municipality for Airbus' first aircraft final assembly line outside Europe.

To Airbus China president Laurence Barron, commercial success and industrial collaboration are equally important. The European aircraft manufacturer picked up speed in developing its industrial partnership with China in 2004 when Barron began leading its business here.

"Airbus set its goal of achieving 50 percent of the Chinese market," Barron recalls. "But we realized that was not very likely to occur unless we could substantially increase our industrial footprint in China," Barron recalls.

"It was a collective decision that we had to make much effort not only in the commercial area, but also in the industrial arena. We needed to substantially increase the procurement from China and develop new ways we cooperate with Chinese counterparts," Barron adds.

Before 2004 Airbus purchased less than US$20 million of its aircraft components per year from Chinese factories. But by the end of 2007, its subcontracting volume to China exceeded US$70 million per year. "Our target was to reach US$120 million per year by 2010. We expect to exceed that target by reaching about US$200 million per year by then and US$450 million per year in 2015," Barron says.

Technicians work in an
Airbus aircraft cockpit.

Industrial cooperation between Airbus and China dates
back to 1985. Aerospatiale, currently Airbus France,
signed the first product subcontracting agreement with
Xi'an Aircraft Company to manufacture and assemble
access doors for Airbus A300/A310 wide-body aircraft.
Currently, six Chinese manufacturers are manufacturing

parts, such as wing components, emergency-exit doors and maintenance tools for Airbus aircraft.

The country has been supplying components to both global leading trunk line aircraft producers such as Boeing and Airbus, and regional aircraft makers such as Embraer and a number of helicopter producers. Over 3,500 Boeing aircraft, or about one-third of Boeing's total fleet in service, are equipped with components produced in China. Half of Airbus worldwide fleet, some 5,000 aircraft, has components made in China. The country is even planning to build its own large commercial aircraft by 2020.

"All this experience means that the Chinese aviation industry is a world player," says Barron. "So it is perfectly normal when we are launching a new program we should include a significant share from China."

He is referring to a plan for China to design five percent of the airframe of the A350XWB, Airbus' latest long-haul model which is due to enter service in 2013. The Airbus (Beijing) Engineering Center will start the bulk of design work for the A350XWB program by the middle of 2008, Barron says. The center is 70 percent owned by Airbus, five percent held by China Aviation Industry Corp I (AVIC I) and 25 percent by AVIC II. It employs 125 engineers and that figure will increase to 200 by the end of 2008.

Airbus also plans to set up a joint venture with Hafei Aviation Industry Co. Ltd., a subsidiary of AVIC II, in Harbin, northeast China's Heilongjiang Province, to produce composite material parts and components for the

A350XWB. The project is expected to begin in the first quarter of 2009.

The A320 final assembly line in Tianjin has been in the spotlight since 2005 when Airbus announced its intention to assemble aircraft in China.

"The final assembly line is one part of a much bigger industrial cooperation program between Airbus and China. But it is the sexiest part of the cooperation. People want to see a plane delivered in China. It is more exciting than seeing a door manufactured here," Barron says.

The single-aisle A320 family aircraft is the most successful model of Airbus. The company now produces about 34 A320 family jets a month and aims to increase that number to 40 a month in 2009.

The Tianjin factory started to assemble the first jet at the end of September and is expected to deliver it in summer 2009. It will be able to roll out four jets a month by the end of 2011.

Barron says that the Chinese government has expressed "strong desire" for the project from the very beginning. The project is expected to provide industrial and management know-how to the Chinese aircraft manufacturing industry. More importantly, it will help Tianjin attract investment from other aviation-related companies for long-term impact on the future development of Tianjin as an economic center of north China.

By LU HAOTING

AmCham-China

AMCHAMP

James Zimmerman,
Chairman of AmCham

For James Zimmerman, Chairman of the American Chamber of Commerce (AmCham) in China, the country's entry into the World Trade Organization (WTO) in 2001 was its most significant change in the past three decades of reform and opening-up.

"After that, China indeed opened up its market and started to integrate into the world economy," says Zimmerman. As AmCham Chairman since 2006, Zimmerman is also a lawyer who had started doing China-related business 20 years ago. Living and working permanently in China for the last seven years, he has witnessed many changes himself.

The number of AmCham members has increased by nearly 10 percent every year during the past years, and Zimmerman is confident that it will maintain the growth rate as long as China remains attractive to investors.

Business opportunities in China have benefited investors at various levels. When AmCham first opened its office in Beijing in 1980, it had a small number of members, and most were multinationals. While the big names are still there today, an increasing number of small and medium-sized enterprises have joined AmCham.

"They are brought here by the vast business opportunities in China," says Zimmerman.

Three decades ago, only a few cities in China were known by the outside world.

When foreigners came, the two choices were overwhelmingly Beijing or Shanghai. Today AmCham members have cast their eyes further, and five years ago AmCham began inviting its members to visit 10 second- and third-tier cities, including Chengdu, Dalian and Shenyang.

"The economy in these cities is developing fast, and the rising middle class there have huge demand of goods and services," says the Chairman.

The dynamic economy also leads to a changing landscape of investment, and the list of cities to be visited keeps increasing. "A third-tier city today could be a second-tier city tomorrow," Zimmerman says. Although its headquarters is still in Beijing, business and members of AmCham are now spread all over the country.

A major role of AmCham is to communicate with Chinese officials on current issues and enhance mutual understanding. AmCham has publicized an annual *White Paper* on doing business in China and handed it over to various Chinese government departments since 1999. Based on surveys among its members, the annual *White Paper* reflects the law enforcement and business environment in China.

AmCham held its 2007 Appreciation Dinner in November 2007. Senior government officials and business leaders, including US Embassy Deputy Chief of Mission Daniel Piccuta (left), Vice Premier Wu Yi(middle), and AmCham Chairman James Zimmerman(right), were present.

As part of networking efforts, AmCham also maintains the tradition of organizing a high-profile annual dinner at the end of each year, inviting high-ranking officials and businessmen. In 2007, Vice Premier Wu Yi delivered the keynote speech on trade relations between China and the US. Among the Chinese officials that he had met, Zimmerman says Wu impressed him most for her integrity and capability of dealing with tough issues.

"We wish there were more Chinese officials like her," Zimmerman says of Wu who was scheduled for retirement after the National People's Congress in 2008.

AmCham members have also been active in Washington, D.C. where they lobbied for most favored nation status for China in the 1990s and were supportive of China's entry into the WTO. Recently, it has been active in communicating with the US side on other issues such as IPR protection, market access, and lowering trade barriers.

As a lawyer, Zimmerman has also witnessed the changes in China's law-making process.

A series of laws, which aim to make doing business in China more regulated, have been put into practice during the past decades. Significant ones include the *Antimonopoly Law* and the *Tax Law*, which gives domestic and foreign investors an equal tax rate. The *Labor Contract Law*, which has caused wide debate and worries that it may drive foreign investors away from China, is also important in terms of labor benefits protection, according to Zimmerman.

"I hope all these laws can be appropriately put into practice," he says.

When asked why he has been here so long, Zimmerman said he has stayed for the opportunities, as well as the challenges in China. Life, as well as work here, keeps changing. When he first came here 10 years ago, the main vehicle in the city was the bicycle. Today, streets are dominated by private cars and the new Beijing Airport Terminal 3 has just begun its test run. China was just opening its door to foreigners and investors when he first came, and Beijing has hosted the Olympics in 2008.

Looking ahead, AmCham believes that China will continue to change, and bilateral trade will bring the two countries even closer.

Meanwhile, Zimmerman says that there are several aspects that he hopes China can improve. Larger market access, a more independent judiciary system and more transparency in the law-making process are something he looks forward to as China carries on its reforms.

By DIAO YING

Johnny Kwan,
Chairman of BASF
Greater China Country
Board

"Honeybee" is the word Johnny Kwan uses to describe his company.

As chairman of BASF Greater China Country Board, Kwan is leading the company's efforts in environmental protection and corporate social responsibility (CSR).

"In the process of honey making, a honeybee is continuously spreading pollen, which will enrich the environment. Then with the pollen more flowers will blossom, and more honey will be made, so everybody is winning," Kwan says.

"In BASF, we are working hard to benefit not only ourselves, but also our stake holders, as well as the industry and the environment," he says.

The German chemical maker originally started its trade with China in 1885. Today, it has become one of the leading foreign investors in the Chinese chemical industry.

With over 6,000 employees in China, BASF currently operates 23 wholly owned subsidiaries and 10 joint ventures in the country. The company's portfolio in China now ranges from chemicals and plastics to agricultural products.

Today China is the company's third largest market, after Germany and the United States. In 2007, the company achieved sales volume of about 4.4 billion euros in the Chinese market.

China is also BASF's fastest growing market globally. "Over the last four years our business has increased three-fold in the country," says Kwan.

Grow with China

BASF products have entered China for more than 100 years. As early as in 1904, China already accounted for seven percent of BASF's global sales, with then synthetic indigo as the company's key product. In 1950, the company was represented by the Hong Kong-based Jebsen & Co. Ltd as its sole agent for trade in China.

Realizing China's importance as a market, BASF in 1982 set up its own subsidiary in Hong Kong, with the name of BASF China Co. Ltd. In the 1980s the company started to set up joint ventures with Chinese partners to expand its presence in the country.

In the early 1990s, the company came up with its "Vision 2010", saying that by the year, 20 percent of the company's global sales will come from Asia Pacific. "What is important in the vision is that half of the 20 percent will come from China," says Kwan.

"What's more, in the Asia-Pacific region, our target is that 70 percent of the sales will come directly with locally-produced goods, and this also applies to China," he says.

With this vision the company started several big manu-facturing projects in China. In December 2000, BASF and Sinopec established a joint venture company, to build and operate an integrated petrochemical site in Nanjing, capital of Jiangsu Province.

Total investment in the project was US$2.9 billion and BASF held a 50 percent stake. It was the company's largest investment in China, as well as its largest single overseas investment in its 140 years of history.

At the core of the integrated site is a steam cracker supply-ing nine world-scale downstream plants. The site can pro-duce about 1.7 million tons of chemicals and polymers per year. All plants began commercial operations in mid-2005.

Following its successful operation both Sinopec and BASF agreed to expand this joint project, with an additional investment of US$900 million. New facilities will come on-stream starting in 2008.

"The Nanjing integrated site has used BASF's most advanced technology. With production in the integrated site, we can save a lot of raw materials and energy, and also centralize our waste treatment and environmental protection," says Kwan. "Globally we have six such inte-grated sites. We can realize about 800 million euros of savings each year from these six sites."

Apart from the Nanjing project BASF also expanded its production facilities in other regions in China. In mid-2006 the company's second biggest project in China, an integrated isocyanates complex, started commercial pro-duction, with the total investment of US$1 billion.

An international diversified team for the BASF Nanjing integrated site.

In China, BASF is quickening its pace in research and development (R&D). It has set up a number of technical centers to improve the company's technology to better suit customers. These centers cover a lot of areas, ranging from automotive gear and footwear to lady's skin care.

The company is also paying a lot of attention to basic research. Started in 1997, the BASF Sino-German R&D fund has supported collaborations with Chinese universities and relevant institutes through grants and scholarships.

"Until now we have been running over 50 research projects under the fund, covering fields like macromolecule material science, organic compounds, industrial catalyst research, nanotechnology and biotechnology," says Kwan.

Future Development

Looking into the future, Kwan says, "organic growth and mergers and acquisitions (M&A) are equally important to BASF in China". Besides a lot of investment in east China, the company is seriously considering making a major investment in the west in Chongqing, to produce MDI, an important chemical raw material.

In some businesses, BASF is also looking for M&A opportunities. For instance, in 2006 the company acquired domestic concrete additives producer, Hi Con. China's construction chemicals industry is growing very fast. The company will take advantage of this to better develop the business, says Kwan.

In the past few years, BASF acquired some companies globally. It bought Degussa's construction chemicals business, acquired Johnson Polymer, as well as the catalysts producer Engelhard.

In China, any M&A deal must match the company's overall strategies, which is to better serve the customers and the environment. With Chinese government putting more emphasis on the environment, the country's chemical industry will see healthier growth in the future, says Kwan.

"In BASF, we are not only doing environmental protection by ourselves, but also promoting it in cooperation with the Chinese government and the industry authorities," he says.

By WAN ZHIHONG

Carrefour

FRENCH CONNECTION

Eric Legros,
President and CEO of
Carrefour China

When Carrefour entered the Chinese market in 1995, the French supermarket chain chose to do it quietly, kind of like testing the water rather than making a splash. There was no marching band or lion dance to announce the opening of its first outlet in Beijing.

It was perhaps premature to be celebrating because nobody was sure whether the Chinese consumers were ready to change their life-long habit of buying groceries from their neighborhood stores for an entirely new shopping experience that de-emphasized any form of human interaction. It was obviously not the Chinese style.

But embrace it they did. Since that rather tepid first foray, Carrefour has opened 116 more stores on the mainland with a total floor area of nearly one million sq. m and is employing almost 50,000 people.

Its adopted Chinese name — *Jia Le Fu* (happy and lucky family in English) — has become practically synonymous with "supermarket" on the mainland. The company's sales in China amounted to 30 billion *yuan* in 2007, accounting for about five percent of total group revenue.

As the first international supermarket in the Chinese market, Carrefour has opened more than 110 outlets in China.

Because of its growth potential, the Chinese market is enjoying almost as much attention from Carrefour's management as the group's home market in France. Two questions are raised invariably at management meetings in the head office, according to Eric Legros, president and CEO of Carrefour China.

One is "How are we doing in France?" and the other is "What have we been doing in China?" Legros says.

Abandoning the leisurely pace of expansion in the first 10 years of exploration in the Chinese market, Carrefour, in 2005, began to step on the throttle and switched into high gear while opening new outlets. In the three years since, the company has opened 60 new stores, the same number opened in the previous 10 years.

A Carrefour supermarket sets up a "dragon boat" just days before Chinese traditional Dragon Boat Festival.

A Carrefour supermarket.

In that rush for expansion, the company has opened more new stores not only in the major cities, but also in the second-tier cities and townships in the central and western regions of the country. For instance, Carrefour has five stores in Chengdu and four stores in Chongqing.

Legros, who became Carrefour's CEO in China in 2006, says he believes the company owes its success in this market not to any fancy marketing strategy, but rather to its dedicated application to its core business model.

"We have four concepts to (operating) supermarket: one-stop shopping, low prices fresh goods, shelf service and free parking," he says.

"The presence of Carrefour has accelerated competitiveness in the Chinese retailing industry, enabling customers to buy goods cheaper than before."

Although the company's business model has remained international, its staff in China has increasingly been localized, which, according to Legros, has greatly contributed to its success.

Although Legros doesn't speak Chinese, he feels quite proud of being treated as "one of them" by his local staff, who call him "*lao zong*", a common Chinese way of addressing one's boss.

"We are very proud of our local employees. We trained and developed 40 to 50 store managers each year, most of them are (from the mainland), who are really very highly qualified," he says, adding that the company owes much of its rapid growth at a rate of 20 to 25 stores by year to its local managers. Indeed, the key word to Carrefour's success is localization.

In the early days in China, most of Carrefour's managers were French and Spanish. At that time, hardly any Chinese people in the retail industry knew how to run a supermarket. "But now, we don't need them (foreign managers) anymore. We have talented people like Dai Wei," Legros says, pointing to his national public affairs director sitting beside him. "I'm so sure that some day, the president of Carrefour China will be a Chinese," he adds.

Carrefour established a Carrefour China Institute (CCI) in Shanghai in 2000 to train Chinese managers. Since then, the school has trained about 15,000 managers who are playing an important role in the fast expansion of Carrefour on the mainland. In 2007, 40,000 employees attended various training programs on an average of 23 training hours for each person per year.

Each year, Carrefour China sends some local managers to Europe for further training to gain greater overseas market knowledge and experience, some of which can be applied in China. "In 2008, 100 percent of the 40 stores' managers we are promoting are Chinese," says Legros.

At the beginning, Carrefour opened in three very different cities in China, Beijing, Shanghai and Shenzhen. The three cities are very far away from each other and had different characteristics. Carrefour had to adapt its stores to the specific needs of the consumers in each city.

That experience has given Carrefour the confidence to expand into other cities. "Now we have 60 percent of our supermarkets in the main cities like Beijing, Shanghai and Nanjing, while the rest are located in the western and northern provinces," Legros says. "We want to strike a balance in store distribution."

In the pursuit of expansion, Carrefour faces different competitors in different cities.

"China is a large country, when we think about the Chinese market, we think of it like Europe. In Europe, you have competitors in Germany, you have good retailers in France, and so on.

"The Chinese market is the same. In Beijing, WuMart is good here, and in Shanghai it's Bailian. In Chongqing it would be New-Century. In any city of China, there is always a very good professional local retailer, who generally has a much bigger market share than us.

"This is why we should localize. We need to adapt in every city we enter in China, because every city has its own feature. Beijing is not the same for us as Shanghai, and other cities," Legros explains.

Carrefour has always believed that a successful supermarket should provide low prices for most items. "There is an international rule: people rich or poor like to buy good products at lower prices," says Jean-Luc Chereau, former CEO of Carrefour China. "For rich people, they will pay less, save money and can spend it for other things, such as traveling, entertainment, or real estate. For poor people, they have no choice but to buy their necessities at the best price."

Legros says,"If you go to Chongqing Carrefour any time of the day, you can find both rich people and poor people shopping for what they need or want. If you go to Beijing's Zhongguancun Carrefour on the weekend, you can also find the same mix of people there. Two months ago we had one million customers in a single day in Carrefour China. The Chinese people have the confidence in us and such confidence is our real asset."

By TUO YANNAN

CATERPILLAR

DIGGING IN

Thomas Bluth,
Chairman of Caterpillar
(China) Investment
Co. Ltd.

Caterpillar (Xuzhou) Ltd., which was established in 1994, spent 10 years to produce the first 5,000 machines. But it then spent 11 months to make the next 5,000 products, and in 2006, it celebrated the production of 25,000 machines.

The plant, in cooperation with Xuzhou Construction Machinery Group, is the first joint venture of the world's leading construction and mining equipment manufacturer Caterpillar in China. Today it has become Caterpillar's largest manufacturing facility of excavators in the country.

In China for over 30 years, Caterpillar has become an integral part of the country's economy.

From agricultural irrigation projects in the northeast to remote oilfields in the northwest, from coal extraction mines in the north to hydroelectric facilities at the Three Gorges in the southwest, Caterpillar equipment delivers the power and performance in demanding working conditions.

At present the company's core products manufactured in China include hydraulic excavators, track-type tractors, motor graders and paving products, large diesel engines used primarily for marine and power generation applications and generator sets. The company also manufactures components at several facilities in China.

"In the past 30 years in China, Caterpillar has developed from an entity with only a sales office to a company with having our entire global business model implemented," says Thomas Bluth, chairman of Caterpillar (China) Investment Co. Ltd.

Growth Strategy

Caterpillar sold its first products to China in 1975 and opened its first office in Beijing in 1978.

In the 1980s, Caterpillar launched technology transfer agreements with several Chinese manufacturers who began building Caterpillar licensed products.

Caterpillar hydraulic excavator.

Caterpillar 160H Motor
Grader.

In 1987 the company signed technology transfer agreements with 12 companies in 10 provinces in China,
which marked another milestone for Caterpillar.

Caterpillar's expansion in China accelerated in the early
1990s with the establishment of a more significant local
production strategy.

Then from the late 1990s the company started to bring
in all the different elements of its business model, such
as financial services, remanufacturing, technology and
logistics.

In 2008 Caterpillar completed its acquisition of Shandong SEM Machinery Co. Ltd., one of China's leading
wheel loader manufacturers.

Commenting on the deal, Bluth says,"Organic growth
accounted for a large part of our development in China,

we also continue to look at opportunities in terms of partnerships as well as acquisitions."

To Caterpillar, the Chinese market is "of critical importance", says Bluth.

"In 2005, our company went through a full review of our business strategy globally. We picked seven critical success factors, and China was one of them."

In 2006, Caterpillar's sales revenue in China was around US$1 billion. "In 2008 the figure will double, and we expect to double it again to US$4 billion by 2010."

Caterpillar excavator broke earth for the "Water Cube" in 2003.

"Compared with the company's global business, which aims to approach US$60 billion by 2010, the Chinese market does not account for a big part, but the growth rate here is tremendous," he says.

The next three years will be very important for Caterpillar in China as the company will see several projects come onstream, and will further increase its investment in the country.

"Over the next three years Caterpillar is going to invest US$1 billion in capital in the emerging markets, and China will take an important share," says Bluth.

China has started to take measures to revitalize its own equipment manufacturing industry, and several domestic companies have begun to eye the foreign market. "It is good for the whole market and the customers," says Bluth.

Sustainable Development

Taking sustainable development as an important theme, Caterpillar is positioned to provide Chinese customers with products that can help to the country achieve a recycling economy.

"Our remanufacturing business well illustrates this," says Bluth.

The company is a global leader in the remanufacturing business, which is a highly sophisticated form of recycling that takes end-of-life components and turns them into like-new products for a fraction of the cost. The technology helps customers remain competitive and promotes a sustainable environment by reducing waste and the need for raw materials to make new parts.

Caterpillar Remanufacturing Services is one of the first wholly-owned foreign entities to receive a remanufacturing license in China.

To support its Chinese customers, dealers and other customers in the Asia-Pacific region, the company has opened a regional remanufacturing center in Shanghai.

The company and the National Development and Reform Commission (NDRC) have signed a letter of intent through which both parties will promote the development of China's remanufacturing industry. As part of the letter of intent, Caterpillar will provide expertise to assist NDRC and Chinese research institutions in supporting the development of the remanufacturing industry in China.

Apart from the remanufacturing business, Caterpillar is also working with Chinese partners in sustainable energy supply. It has supplied 60 gas generator sets to Sihe Coal Mine in Jincheng in Shanxi Province, to burn coal methane to generate electricity.

The methane gas power project, developed by Shanxi Jincheng Anthracite Coal Mining Group Co.Ltd., is the largest of its kind in the world. The project will have a capacity of 120 MW, providing a new source of electricity generated from a fuel source that was once considered a waste product. According to Caterpillar statistics, the

Sihe Project is expected to reduce greenhouse gas emission by 4.5 million tons over a 20-year period and serve as a model for future Clean Development Mechanism projects in China using coalbed methane.

China and the US have agreed during the second Strategic Economic Dialogue in May 2007 to develop up to 15 large-scale coalmine methane capture and utilization projects in China in the next five years.

"Caterpillar has been working to help customers all over the world develop integrated power solutions. The Sihe Project is important and we are confident that it will be successful," says Bluth.

"The use of Caterpillar engines is a great example of how Caterpillar products and technology can be used to help China reach its environmental goals," he says.

By WAN ZHIHONG

REACHING OUT

Few multinational CEOs would come to China twice in one year. But John Chambers, chairman and CEO of Cisco Systems, came to China three times in the past seven months.

In his latest visit to Sichuan Province in July 2008, Chambers announced Cisco would donate 300 million *yuan* to the relief work and reconstruction for the May 12 earthquake, making him one of the few foreign CEOs

Cisco's headquarters in San Jose, California, USA.

who came to visit the disrupted areas shortly after the disaster.

Although it was one of Chambers' several visits to China since the company entered the country in 1994, Thomas Lam, president of Cisco China, contends that Chambers' latest visit to Sichuan Province had the most significant impact on the company's development in the country.

Thomas Lam,
President
of Cisco China

"It is like making friends. First, it is all about business. Then you'll feel that it is also about feelings and connections," says Lam. "In John's latest visit to Sichuan, I saw almost emotional things. I think that will help Cisco become not only business partner but a life-time friend to China."

As the world leader in networking that transforms how people connect, communicate and collaborate, Cisco's China story started in August 1994 when the company opened its first office selling routers and switchers.

The company later opened another office in Shanghai in 1995 and two offices in Guangzhou and Chengdu in 1996 as the business grew. In 1998, Cisco established its Chinese subsidiary company and a networking technology lab in Beijing.

However, the company did not have much investment in China until 2005 when it opened the Cisco China R&D Center in Shanghai as one of the major parts of its global R&D capacities.

"In the earlier years, China's Internet was dominated by entertainment applications and there were only a few applications or services for business," says Lam.

"But the rise of Web 2.0 technology has changed the market since three to four years ago and that has significantly boosted the application of network in business here."

Sensing the market opportunity, Lam, who joined Cisco in 1998, started to accelerate the company's pace in the country and made an adjustment to Cisco China's organization.

"Since 1994, Cisco China worked in an organization in which people were focusing on a number of vertical industries," says Lam. "In 2006 I changed the whole organization into four national regions while keeping our overall focus on vertical industries, which flattens our organization and shortens our distance from customers."

Boosted by the restructuring, Cisco's revenue surged about 40 percent in 2006, much higher than the 20 percent average growth rate in the Asia Pacific.

US$16 billion Investment

Cisco's development in China came into a climax in November 2007 when Chambers announced Cisco would invest US$16 billion in the next three to five years to expand its procurement, manufacturing as well as R&D capacity in China.

The investment startled many as it is nearly twice the company's US$7.3 billion net income in 2007.

"The announcement underscored both China's strategic importance to Cisco's global operations and the broad range of growth opportunities presented by the Chinese market, particularly as an innovator in the next wave of the Internet's development in collaboration and Web 2.0 technology," says Chambers. "This program will lay the foundation for the next chapter of Cisco's development in China."

However, Lam contends that he did not expect his boss to announce the plan so quickly. "He got off the plane at 4 am that day," recalls Lam. "Before that he told me he was just looking around this time and would decide whether to increase our investment in China when he went back to the United States. But just hours after he came to China, he changed his mind."

In fact, what Chambers saw in China was amazing. By the end of 2007, Internet users in China reached 210 million, an increase of 53.3 percent year on year, according to statistics from China Internet Network Information Center (CNNIC).

But China's Internet penetration, which stands at 16 percent, is still lower than the world average of 19.1 percent, which means the country still has a huge potential demand for network-related products and services in the following years. "As more Chinese companies want to become as competitive as their foreign peers, they will start investing in their IT systems and networks," says Lam.

"In fact, most of our Chinese customers are more willing to adopt new products and applications than their foreign peers since they do not have much previous IT investment to worry about."

Encouraged by the opportunities, Cisco started to aggressively expand in the Chinese market. The company announced in April the establishment of the "Cisco China Strategy Board", a cross-functional executive board of senior leaders across Cisco's global business.

It also appointed Jim Sherriff, Cisco's senior vice-president of global operations, to a newly formed position of chairman of Cisco China in an effort to inject Cisco's global resources into the campaign.

In addition, the company signed memorandum of understandings with China's National Development and Reform Commission (NDRC) and Ministry of Commerce to boost innovation and information technology development in the country. It also formed partnerships with Chinese companies including e-commerce giant Alibaba Group and home applicance maker Haier to expand its business scope in the country.

"We hope to become a life-time friend with China, not just business partners, so we need a wide range of partnerships in the country," says Lam. "In the future, we will spend more time in looking for new market opportunities here and make ourselves grow with the country."

By WANG XING

Deloitte Touche Tohmatsu

NUMBER CRUNCHING

James H. Quigley, who was named chief executive officer (CEO) of Deloitte Touche Tohmatsu in June 2007, has visited China four times since he took the new position.

In the past nine months, Quigley also visited Moscow and Sao Paulo, but China has been a prominent destination. "I believe what is happening here (in China) will bring Deloitte and our clients huge opportunities," he says.

Deloitte Touche
Tohmatsu's Beijing
office.

Indeed, the firm says it will spare no effort to capture this opportunity. In 2004, Deloitte unveiled a five-year China growth strategy, which included an investment of US$150 million in China, a 400 percent staff increase and a plan to increase revenue four to five fold.

However, unlike many multinational companies that witnessed decades of exuberant growth after the country opened its gate to the rest of the world in 1978, top executives at Deloitte believe that their story in China is just beginning.

James H. Quigley,
CEO of Deloitte
Touche Tohmatsu

In fact, the international accounting firm's business in China grew relatively slowly in the first decade after 1978. It was not until the beginning of the 1990s, when the Chinese government started to build a modern enterprise system necessary for the growth of China's market-oriented economy, did global accounting firms see a significant role to play.

Along with the reform of the State-owned enterprises, China started a series of reforms that saw the convergence of its accounting standards with international practice. The accounting standards reform provided business opportunities for international accounting firms who were experienced with the international standards.

In December 1992, Deloitte established its first mainland office in Shanghai. In the same year, another major global accounting firm, Ernst & Young, established its first mainland office in Beijing through a partnership with a local firm.

By the end of the 1990s, 11 international accounting firms had set up 26 offices in the Chinese mainland but the market share was dominated by the top five global accounting firms, Deloitte, Arthur Anderson, Pricewaterhouse Cooper, KPMG and Ernst & Young.

Comparatively, local accounting firms still remained on a small scale, with each firm having an average of 20 staffers and limited services.

International accounting firms reached another milestone when China joined the World Trade Organization in December 2001.

Deloitte Touche Tohmatsu office building.

Accounting service businesses developed quickly in the post-WTO years, along with increased mergers and acquisitions and on-shore and offshore initial public offerings conducted by Chinese companies.

For example, 10 years ago, Deloitte China accounted for about one percent of the total number of employees of its global network. Now it accounts for five percent.

But Peter Bowie, Senior Partner of Deloitte China thinks the firm is still in "a very very early stage."

Indeed, Deloitte has every reason to consider its future in China to be bright. As Quigley pointed out, in the United States, Deloitte has some 40,000 staff. It has over 8,000 staff here in China.

"Considering China's economic growth, the business opportunity is critical to us," he says.

Deloitte is hoping to tap the development potential of the service industry in China, which only accounts for 40 percent of GDP, compared to 70 percent in some developed countries.

"Some people want to characterize China as the world's factory and I think that is not what China is going to be," Quigley says. "The economy will begin to take on a much more diverse growth where services will play an increasingly important role, while manufacturing will continue to be dominant. The growth of Deloitte is evidence of that."

Looking at China's capital market and capitalization, professional services such as accounting services and legal services are benefiting from a broad range of financial services.

"If you just look at the capital market in the emerging economies, you'll see very significant services are building up around it," Quigley says.

Even though the markets are suffering serious corrections as a result of the US credit crunch, Deloitte's top executives remain confident.

"Surely, the downturn in the United States will affect Europe and China. I think it will probably last another eight to 18 months. But we are investing in the long term growth of China. You cannot turn on and off because the market is too big in terms of opportunity," Bowie says. "It is not a short term decision."

Deloitte is not alone in capitalizing on the opportunity. Other leading accounting firms such as Ernst & Young and PricewaterhouseCoopers, all have ambitious recruitment plans in China.

For example, both Ernst & Young and PricewaterhouseCoopers initiated plans to recruit around 10,000 new staffers in China in five years beginning in 2006.

However, for accounting service companies the talent challenge can't be ignored.

"The talent challenge exists on a global basis and it is even more severe here," Quigley says. "So our ability to develop and retain people is going to be the source of our sustained competitive advantage."

From Deloitte's perspective, talent shortage is a problem not at the entry level, but at the experience level. "The challenge becomes that you grow so fast and people in the middle with experience will be in a great demand," Bowie says.

To address the challenge, Deloitte plans to bring in 40 new local partners in the next six months.

That is part of the reason why both Quigley and Bowie denied calling the firm a multinational company (MNC), since 92 percent of the partners in Deloitte China are from China.

"The company is different from a MNC. Rather, as a firm in partnership, Deloitte China is a member firm of Deloitte Global," Bowie says.

"We are local," Quigley adds. "It is not that we think we are local; we are local. That is even a theme we are using to drive our strategy."

At Deloitte, the approach is called "local roots and global connections".

"We understand the language and culture," Quigley adds. "In addition to the local roots, Deloitte has global connections to give our staff a window to the world and our clients access seamless client service anywhere in the world. It gives us access to a very powerful network of professionals, namely, 165,000 professionals on a global basis."

By ZHANG RAN

Milestones

1917: Shanghai office opened, becoming the first foreign accounting organization to establish a presence in the city.

1989: Deloitte Touche Tohmatsu was formed as a result of the merger between Deloitte Haskins & Sells International and Touche Ross International.

December 1992: Deloitte Touche Tohmatsu Certified Public Accountants Ltd. was established in Shanghai.

1997: Deloitte Touche Tohmatsu merged with Kwan Wong Tan and Fong, the largest Chinese firm of Certified Public Accountants in Hong Kong SAR.

June 1998: Deloitte Touche Tohmatsu Certified Public Accountants Ltd. Beijing Branch was established.

June 1, 2004: A five year China growth strategy was unveiled that earmarked a US$150 million investment in China to increase staff by 400 percent, and revenue four to five fold. Moreover, the firm unveiled its new global brand in China and announced its Beijing office relocation to the Oriental Plaza.

June 1, 2005: The firm had its first ever merger in the Chinese Mainland with Beijing Pan-China CPA Ltd. On September 1 the firm merged with Pan-China Schinda. This was the second merger for Deloitte in the Chinese Mainland.

Today: The company has over 8,000 employees in 10 cities including Beijing, Dalian, Guangzhou, Hong Kong, Macao, Nanjing, Shanghai, Shenzhen, Suzhou and Tianjin.

EU

THRIVING PARTNERSHIP

Serge Abou,
Ambassador of
Delegation of the
European Commission

China's relationship with the European Union (EU) is so well established that even the Ambassador of Delegation of the European Commission Serge Abou barely recalls the first trade agreement between China and the former European Economic Community signed in 1978. "It's archeology," he jokes. "I have to check it in the archive."

The agreement, which was signed the year China began its reform and opening-up policy, was also the first pact between the two sides after they established diplomatic relations in 1975. According to the agreement, the two granted each other most favored nation status and took measures to encourage bilateral trade flows. This included the creation of a EU-China Joint Committee.

The agreement concentrated on trade that ushered in an era of bilateral economic cooperation between the two economies. From being almost non-existent 30 years ago, two-way trade between the EU and China reached US$356.15 billion in 2007. Abou says it took the two parties seven years to formalize the agreement, which originally had been scheduled to take effect in five years.

A trade and economic agreement signed in 1985 later replaced the 1978 pact. Under the framework of this agreement the EU-China relationship developed in every sector. "Now, there is no one single domain where we have no cooperation," Abou says. "We now have intense individual contact, person-to-person, company-to-company, suppliers-to-buyers and investors-to-partners. We also have cooperation in research and higher education."

There are over 20 so-called sectoral dialogues, which annually bring together ministerial-level personnel from China and Europe. China and the EU are also partners in the Galileo project — a co-operative satellite navigation initiative — and a research nuclear reactor program.

When Abou took his position as EU ambassador to China in 2005, China and the European economic bloc were preparing to update the 1985 trade agreement and formal talks finally began in 2007.

According to Abou, the latest round of talks in Beijing was "progressing". "In the next summit, which will probably take place in December in France, we expect there will be an earlier harvest of chapters. The important thing is to make it a wise and wide-ranging agreement," he adds. The talks will include general topics of political and economic nature and cooperation and policy discussions. Also on the agenda are exchanges on technical issues such as the protection of intellectual property rights, trade disputes and environmental protection policies.

Disputes occur between intimate trade partners, too. As the EU becomes the largest trade partner of China and China the second largest of the EU, conflicts, such as anti-dumping and technical trade barriers are also increasing.

Talking about how to strengthen the economic ties, Abou expects Beijing to give foreign investors larger access to service sectors such as insurance, banking, and telecommunications that are currently restricted for outsiders for the most part. He also urges China to enhance its protection of intellectual property rights and trade facilitation.

"Sometimes, Chinese may have the impression that their investments are not welcomed in Europe. It is totally wrong," the ambassador says. He adds Chinese investors are "very welcome" in almost all industries in the EU except for those linked to national security, which is normal in every country in the world.

Looking back at China's achievement in the past 30 years, Abou says what impresses him most is not the marvelous figures in GDP, trade or foreign reserves but changes for each individual Chinese. "That is a fundamental change," he says. "In 30 years all the categories of population are improving."

He explains there are hundreds of millions of people who have been saved from poverty. And Chinese people have better housing, better transportation, and better opportunities for jobs and education, as well as better opportunities to travel. "In the mind of every young Chinese today, there is hope that his or her future will be better," he says.

By JIANG WEI and FU YU

Milestones

May 1975: Diplomatic relations established after a visit of European Commissioner Christopher Soames.

April 1978: European Commission (EC) and China signed a trade agreement in Brussels.

May 1985: The EC and China signed Trade and Economic Cooperation Agreement in Brussels.

October 1988: A delegation of the EC began its operation in Beijing.

April 1998: The First European Union (EU)-China Summit took place in London. The EC adopted a policy paper on *Building a Comprehensive Partnership with China*.

May 2000: The EU and China concluded bilateral negotiations on China's accession to the World Trade Organization.

June 2001: The EC released a Communique entitled *EU Strategy Towards China: Implementation of the 1998 Communication and Future Steps for a More Effective EU Policy*.

October 2003: The Sixth EU-China Summit took place in Beijing. The summit was the first occasion for leaders from both sides to meet since China issued its policy paper on EU relations, and the EU approved its strategy for relations with China in the coming years.

February 2004: The EU and China signed the milestone Approved Destination Status Agreement.

September 2005: The Eighth EU-China summit was held in Beijing. Agreements on various sectors were signed.

October 2006: The European Commission adopted a new China strategy paper and a working document on trade and investment, which reframed the EU's approach to its partnership with China.

January 2007: EU Commissioner Benita Ferrero-Waldner visited China for the official launch of negotiations on a Comprehensive Partnership and Cooperation Agreement.

FUJIFILM
CHINA FOCUS

Many major Japanese companies seem to coincide their China entries with Chinese State leaders' visits to Japan.

In 1978, when China embraced the reform and opening-up policy, Japan was the destination for many State leaders who were eager to introduce advanced technology and management practices to jumpstart China's stagnant economy. A visit by Deng Xiaoping to Panasonic in 1978 sparked the Japanese conglomerate's investment in China and another factory tour to Canon in 1979 by Deng Yingchao, the widow of late Premier Zhou Enlai, was a prelude to the precision equipment maker's foray into China.

So when former Vice-premier Yao Yilin visited Fujifilm in 1983, it seemed a bit late for the film maker, which launched its first China office only in 1984.

Fujifilm caught the slow boat to China but it was not un-charted waters, according to Koji Yokota, who holds the helm for the firm's China operation. "In terms of direct investment, we lagged behind (other Japanese firms). But we were one of the very first to do business with China," he says.

In 1963, Fujifilm sent a group of technicians to China to investigate the local cinefilm and X-ray film market and in the following year their Chinese counterparts paid return visits to Fujifilm. After that the firm began exporting cinefilm, print film, color film, X-ray film and photography equipment to China.

That gave Fujifilm the upper hand even though its direct investment didn't start until the 1990s. Years of brand penetration made Fujifilm a Chinese household name in the late 1980s when cameras and film became affordable for an increasing number of Chinese, thanks to the reform and opening-up policy.

"We adopted a three-step strategy in China," Yokota says. "First, we dealt with exports and imports with the country. Then we started direct investment in China in the 1990s by setting up factories. Third, in 2001 we established regional headquarters in China and started

During the late 1980s and mid-1990s, Fujifilm dominated China's film market and its green packaging became an industry icon.

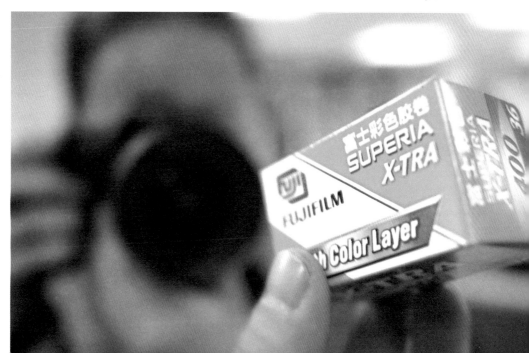

running our local business as a strategic market. All these steps are in line with the process of China's reform and opening-up. I think every step was steady and well-researched and planned."

Green vs. Yellow

During the late 1980s and mid-1990s, Fujifilm dominated China's film market and for a time its share reached as high as 70 percent. Its green packaging became an industry icon.

However, it found the Chinese market chilly by 1998. At that time, all seven major local film makers were in the red with combined losses of billions of dollars. With a planned economy still dogging China, the government was eager to turn the corner by pushing local companies to form joint ventures. Fujifilm was already negotiating with a Shanghai company to form a joint venture in hopes of localizing its film manufacturing. But Eastman Kodak was more aggressive.

With an endorsement from Chinese Premier Zhu Rongji, Ying Yeh, the chief negotiator for Kodak and former US diplomat, finally sealed an exclusive deal with the Chinese government under which Kodak would form joint ventures with six of the seven major local companies.

That marked a big setback for Fujifilm by putting the brakes to its localization efforts. The firm, in 1994, set up a factory in Tianjin to produce lenses, followed by a factory in Suzhou in 1995 for cameras. In 2001, it founded a print sheet manufacturing facility in Hebei

Province. It had been counting on a joint venture to locally produce film.

Fujifilm's plan was disrupted by the exclusive deal and Kodak's yellow packaging started to prevail in China. Localization was crucial as duties on imported film were as high as 67 percent before China's entry into the World Trade Organization in 2001. After the deal was signed between the Chinese government and Kodak, Fujifilm's market share dropped to around 10 percent in 2005.

Windfall out of Woes

However, Kodak soon stumbled in its sprawling traditional film manufacturing businesses as cameras went digital.

For Fujifilm, it presented a windfall. "The agreement in 1998 (between Kodak and the Chinese government) was an outcome within a very unique historical context," says Yokota, who was head of Fujifilm's Beijing office when the agreement was signed. "It's true we lost the opportunity to invest in traditional film manufacturing in China, but it also gave us an opportunity to make a digital maneuver." Fujifilm's Suzhou factory began producing digital cameras in 1997, a year before the exclusive deal was signed between Kodak and the Chinese government.

In 2005, Shigetaka Komori, president and CEO of Fujifilm, announced that the Suzhou plant would replace its facility in Japan, to make the firm's largest digital camera production base in the world.

In 2007 the company announced it would fully transfer its digital camera production from Japan to China. That has helped the firm stay a step ahead of Kodak at a time when digital photography prevails.

Now Fujifilm is the world's fourth largest digital camera-maker, the world's biggest supplier of specialized film for liquid-crystal-display screens and leading producer of image-sensing chips used in digital cameras and camera phones.

In China's consumer digital camera market, Fujifilm still lags Sony and Canon, partly because its designs failed to meet local tastes and its marketing campaigns were not aggressive enough. Yokota, who became Fujifilm's China chief in 2006, is now revamping the firm's design and sales pitch to boost market share.

However, digital photography is not the only thing Yokota is counting on to boost sales in China. In fact, digital imaging accounts for only about 20 percent of Fujifilm's total revenues, with information technology and document processing making up the remaining.

In 2006, Fujifilm announced it would form a US$267 million joint venture with Shanghai-based SVA Electron Co. to make colour filters used in liquid crystal displays. That came at a time when many Japanese companies tried to consolidate their China operations by reducing the number of joint ventures in the country.

"Whether it's a joint venture or a wholly-owned subsidiary, we are growing with China, which has become a strategic market for Fujifilm," says Yokota, adding that

Fujifilm has invested more than US$300 million in China since it entered the country.

Seizing a Photo Opportunity

Fujifilm's Koji Yokota's connections with China have helped the Japanese photography firm to thrive in this country.

Koji Yokota's career has been bound with China.

Koji Yokota,
President of Fujifilm
China

In 1986, when many of his colleagues were competing for a chance to study in the United States and Europe, Yokota, who had been working at Fujifilm for 11 years, decided to take Chinese-language courses because of his strong interest in China and his belief in China's market potential.

In 1988, he enrolled in Fudan University in Shanghai to learn Chinese, becoming just the second Fujifilm employee to study in China. Since then he has worked at Fujifilm's offices in Hong Kong and Beijing and at the export division of the company's headquarters in Japan. Since his appointment as general manager of Fujifilm Starlight, a subsidiary of Fujifilm in China, he has turned the printing sheet maker into one of Fujifilm China's most profitable businesses.

Yokota, who became president of Fujifilm China in July 2006, speaks fluent Chinese and is one of the few Japanese who have a keen understanding of the Chinese market and culture and has skillfully combined Japanese and Chinese management styles and practices.

In an interview with *China Business Weekly* reporter, Koji Yokota shares his insight about China's reform and opening-up policy and its impact on Fujifilm's business in the country.

Q: China and Japan share many cultural similarities. And you were one of the first Japanese to come to China to study Chinese after China embraced the reform and opening-up policy. How did the influence of Chinese culture help your career development?

A: Historically, Chinese culture has significantly impacted Japanese people's mentality. Even some Japanese cultural practices were based on those imported from China. Since I came to China, I've met a lot of Chinese people and I believe we share many similarities.

However, compared to Japanese, Chinese tend to think with a more global perspective. Japan is a country with a single ethnic group and as a result Japanese people tend to assume other people should think in a similar way as theirs. For Chinese that's totally different. China is a country with a variety of ethnic groups and naturally Chinese have learned to observe and think in multiple ways and angles.

I think I have learned how to think with a global perspective, a paramount quality for those working at multinationals. That is one of the most important things I have learned since I came to China.

Q: How has Japanese management style and practices impacted Fujifilm's partners in China?

A: First, quality. I have been adhering to quality management (in running our China operations). If we are not able to manufacture products with the same quality standard as that in Japan, we would betray Chinese consumers' trust.

Second, I would say integrity. Japanese people uphold the tacit of understanding between partners, mutual trust and long-term cooperation. Fujifilm's printing business has recorded robust sales. That's the result of the cooperation between Fujifilm and its partners in China's printing industry based on such management ideas.

Q: How did China's reform and opening-up policy impact Fujifilm's business?

A: First, the reform and opening-up policy created sound opportunities for multinationals to enter the Chinese market. Second, the policy has helped Chinese people become richer and hence created a market with huge potential, which has laid a solid foundation for multinationals to expand their businesses in the country. Third, it helped integrate China into the global economy, making the country a major part of multinationals' global operations.

Q: Your own career was closely linked with China's reform and opening-up. Looking back to your 20-year career in China, what impressed you most?

A: The economic boom significantly changed Chinese people's mindsets as well as the social guidelines and laws. Many Chinese people have achieved success on their own. That is totally different from 20 years ago. I'm glad that there are more and more understanding

GROWING
W I T H
CHINA
MNC EXECUTIVES
TALK ABOUT CHINA

100

among Chinese business people. But secondly, I have been urging on myself to work harder or I would lose to them.

Q: You have met many government officials and regulators in the past 20 years. In your view, how did the reform and opening-up policy influence decision-makers and regulators in the country?

A: I think they have developed a global perspective and are becoming more and more open.

Q: And what improvement should be made?

A: They should change their perceptions about foreign-invested companies. I hope they will not treat foreign-invested companies simply as foreign entities. We are also part of Chinese companies.

By LI WEITAO

GE

RISING TOGETHER

GROWING
W I T H
CHINA
MNC EXECUTIVES
TALK ABOUT CHINA
102

Nearly every major economic development in China has benefited General Electric, or GE, the multinational American technology and services conglomerate during its last 17 years in China. GE established its first joint venture in Beijing in 1991, when it opened GE Hangwei Medical Systems Co. in Beijing.

But prior to its re-entry into China in 1991, GE was doing business as early as 1906. The first GE lighting plant in China was built in Shenyang, capital city of northeast China's Liaoning Province, in 1908. And the first coal power turbine generator installed by GE in China in 1921 was still in use in Shanghai until 2004.

But GE's first and biggest break in China came in 2001 when the company received a large order for gas turbines and China also began purchasing an increasing number of aircraft engines from GE.

"The year of 2001 is kind of key inflection point, when things really started to accelerate on the growth side," says Steve Bertamini, chairman and CEO of GE Northeast Asia and China.

Ever since its entry into China, the company has been expanding into many industries, including infrastructure, power generation, aircrafts, healthcare and financial services. In 2003, GE Plastics opened the US$64 million China Technology Center in Zhangjiang Hi-tech Park in Shanghai, one of its four global research and development facilities.

Until 2007, plastic was once GE's largest business in China. As a leading global supplier of hi-tech plastics resin for a broad variety of industries including automotive, healthcare and others, GE Plastics' sales revenue exceeded US$1 billion in China in 2005. GE sold the plastics business in 2007 to SABIC (Saudi Basic Industries Corporation), one of the world's leading manufacturers

GE China Technology
Center in Shanghai
Zhangjiang Hi-tech Park.

of plastics, chemicals, fertilizers and metals, for US$11.6 billion.

GE is also looking to expand its reach to financial services in China in the coming three or five years. "The major gaps, we have today between this market and that in the US are financial services," Bertamini says.

"Financial services, if you look at GE globally, are roughly 45 to 50 percent of our revenues, but we have very small base in China."

With private label credit and auto loans, GE's consumer finance operation, GE Money, is looking for a local partner to complement its global experiences, according to Bertamini.

So far, since 2005 GE Money has worked with the Shenzhen Development Bank to provide credit card services. "Financial service is still in its early stage in China and this is a long game," says Bertamini.

According to the CEO, permission for foreign companies to buy major stakes in Chinese banks is the regulatory constraint that GE would like most to be removed. "There are still a lot of restrictions on the ability for foreign companies to buy majority stakes," says Bertamini. "It's the No. 1 area that will give us flexibility."

In view of the emerging aviation market in China, aircraft leasing is playing an increasingly important role in GE's business expansion.

"Aircraft leasing is a huge market for us," he says. GE owns 120 airplanes in China. "We lease to the major airlines, and we will see the aviation market continue to grow in China," he adds.

During the past decade, GE has also made great efforts to boost its branding in China. "I think in China you recognize a brand's reputation is very important," Bertamini says. GE is also focusing on making a reputation for itself as an eco-friendly company.

"We would like people to associate GE with 'green' and as a company that is interested in environmental protection," he says.

Bertamini says the biggest environment related project GE has operated in China so far is water reuse and recycling system and facility.

In 2004, GE set up the first facility that produces water treatment chemicals in Wuxi of Jiangsu Province, and is now expanding the faci-lity to introduce advanced membrane technologies that are critical to the wasterwater treatment process.

As a worldwide partner of the Olympic Games, GE has also provided core technologies for China's first rainwater recycling system in a major public building at the National Stadium in Beijing.

To date, GE is involved in more than 335 projects related to the Beijing Olympic Games ranging from transportation, security, energy and water to healthcare and lighting.

Looking ahead, Bertamini says, "We are moving more to second-tier cities and even third-tier cities, because future growth is expected to be in the next 10 or 15 years, as people move from rural agricultural sectors to cities. This will create huge demand. You need more hospitals, more roads, more airports, more power and more water. Those are all opportunities for companies to be very well positioned to take advantage of the huge demand."

By WANG LAN

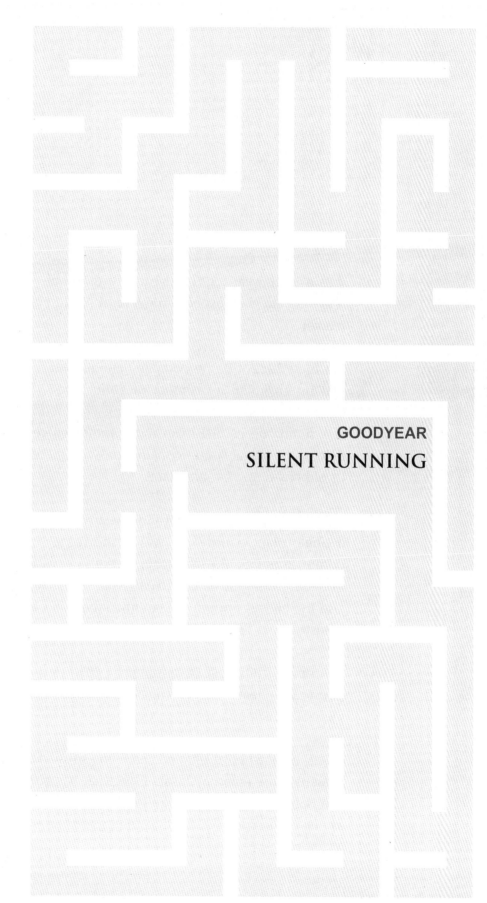

GOODYEAR
SILENT RUNNING

GROWING
W I T H
CHINA
MNC EXECUTIVES
TALK ABOUT CHINA

108

It's a good year for Goodyear Tire & Rubber Co., and the US tire giant expects to roll for more in the Chinese market.

On June 26, 2008, the company announced that it was making an initial investment of about US$500 million for a new plant in Dalian, Liaoning Province, where it was setting up its first mainland commercial vehicle tire manufacturing facility in conjunction with the closure of its old passenger car tire plant.

"It's the biggest investment Goodyear has plunged into a single plant worldwide, which shows our long-term commitment to the Chinese market," says Pierre E. Cohade, president of Goodyear Asia-Pacific region. It's also the biggest one-off foreign investment in China's tire industry.

The new facility will be finished in 2010 and will help boost Goodyear's business in the world's biggest commercial vehicle market.

Since 1994 when it entered the Chinese market with a passenger tire plant in Dalian, Goodyear has built a positive brand image in China and strengthened its foothold as one of the country's top three tire brands, transferring its focus from the OEM (original equipment manufacturing) market to the replacement market in 2005. Its new entry into the commercial vehicle tire segment is driven by China's booming logistics industry.

In September 1994, Goodyear became the first international company to invest in the mainland when it established the Goodyear Dalian Tire Co. Ltd. That year the number of private cars in China was 2.05 million units, which accounted for 21 percent of total passenger cars, and the local auto market was just beginning to boom.

"At that time we focused on the OEM market and supplied international and local carmakers with high quality tires," says Cohade. As more global automakers have set up manufacturing facilities here, the demand for tires has soared.

As a world leader, Goodyear provides tires for nearly all international vehicle brands. "As they come to China one by one, our business grows," says Cohade.

Its global rival French-based Michelin invested in its first joint venture in Shenyang, capital of Liaoning Province, in 1995, while another competitor Bridgestone, from Japan, inaugurated its China plant in the same city in 1999.

In 2004, "when I made the first decision for Goodyear with my boss, we had to choose a new location for Goodyear Asia-Pacific headquarters (which had been in the US); then the question came: 'where is the future (of the tire industry)? '" recalls Cohade.

"We visited Singapore, and Hong Kong. But we found the future was here — Chinese mainland," he adds.

And after traveling to Beijing, Shanghai and Dalian, a new question arrived: "Where is the marketplace?" says Cohade. "I quickly answered, 'Shanghai'."

Cohade says he was impressed by Shanghai's growth and still remembered when he first visited Shanghai in 1996, "the only tall building in Pudong was the Shangri-la Hotel". However three years later upon his second visit, "many buildings stood there, and one couldn't even see the Shangri-la".

Goodyear's newest line of premium passenger tire Assurance for comfort and traction in any weather was launched in the Chinese market in May 2008.

Goodyear made the final decision in 2004 and officially transferred its Asia-Pacific headquarters to Shanghai on April 1, 2005, as part of a major initiative to reinforce its presence in China and the region.

Shifting Focus

China's auto industry exploded in 2002 and 2003, with production hikes of 39.27 and 36.68 percent respectively.

That was good news for Goodyear, which figured that by 2005 millions of those vehicles would need new tires, and the company expected the demand to grow.

On July 5, 2005, Goodyear announced a new development strategy of building a network of retail stores and service centers and the first Goodyear authorized service center was opened in Shanghai.

"As the market changed at the beginning of the new millennium we adjusted our strategy and put more emphasis on the replacement market to become more consumer focused," says Cohade.

The company hired former executives from Eastman Kodak as its president, Asia-Pacific president and China president.

Its retail expansion grew fast and at one point during a short period Goodyear was opening two stores daily.

Currently it has 50 dealerships and more than 800 retail stores nationwide.

A 45.7-m-long Goodyear Blimp flies over Huangpu River, a landmark in Shanghai. Goodyear Blimp is one of the best-known advertising vehicles in the United States, along with the icons of Coca-Cola and McDonald's. In September 2006, the Blimp began its cruise around China.

In March 2006, the company unveiled a service program — the Auto Nurserymaid Plan — free of charge and open to all tire owners. The plan included free puncture repair, a tire care package and exclusive VIP services.

"Along with the development of the industry, competition in the tire market has shifted from price to service. Consumers need comprehensive, customized services, and service is the key to winning in the replacement segment," says Cohade.

Goodyear's other initiative to boost its branding in China's retail market was its iconic symbol, the Goodyear Blimp. As one of the most familiar advertising vehicles in the US (it rivals the icons of Coca-Cola and McDonald's), the first blimp was launched in the US in 1925.

The airship has since flown in many countries, but its maiden flight in China was on September 1, 2006, when the 45.7-meter blimp lifted silently off in Guangdong Province. It was named Navigator in a mainland Internet contest that drew 900 entries.

Navigator was leased from a Florida company called Lightship, which also had a branch in Singapore where the airship, its pilot, co-pilot and 20-person ground crew were also based.

The initial six-week flights throughout Guangdong Province were debut promotional efforts to expand the brand to Chinese drivers who were in the market for new tires.

"Brand and brand image are very important," says former Goodyear spokesman and senior vice-president of global communications Chuck Sinclair. "That was one of the reasons we turned to this global icon."

But explaining the iconography and history of the Goodyear — or *gu te yi* in Mandarin — Blimp to the curious Chinese media required "quite a bit of background", Sinclair says.

But since 2007 the Goodyear Blimp sailed well in various marketing campaigns to promote safe driving around the country, reaching millions of people in Wenzhou, Ningbo, Hangzhou, Shanghai, Suzhou, Shenyang, Dalian, Tianjin, Qingdao, Jinan, Changsha, Shenzhen, Wuhan, and Zhengzhou, among others.

"China has three percent of the world's population of cars," says Cohade. "When we inspected one million cars in Shanghai for free, we surprisingly discovered 30 percent of the tires with problems which might cause accidents."

GROWING
W I T H
CHINA
MNC EXECUTIVES
TALK ABOUT CHINA

114

"I hope we can make a difference by raising customers' safety awareness: when they buy tires, safety will be their first consideration. Moreover, the blimp helps raise Goodyear brand's recognition," he adds.

The promotion has already paid off. Huang Yuling, a staff member of Car Space Service Union, one of Goodyear's leading outlets in Guangzhou, says that after the blimp's appearance, "sales quintupled and shoppers increased by 50 percent. In the next three months, the sales should keep growing at 10 to 15 percent. They know the blimp. Now they know our store."

Cohade declines to disclose the current proportion of Goodyear's OEM and replacement businesses. "China's whole tire industry has shifted from that OEM sector double-sized replacement to the present equal size. Goodyear is higher than the average."

New Markets

After Goodyear reinforced its leadership in both the OEM and replacement markets, it is now looking for growth driven by new markets.

For the past three years, transportation, mostly by trucks, has become busier while many industries have expanded their distribution networks in China.

"In the next five years, transportation (logistics) will see significant growth here," Cohade says.

Currently, its commercial business in China is supplied

Pierre E. Cohade,
President of Goodyear
Asia-Pacific region

by imports, as its old Dalian plant — which is closing down — only produces passenger and light truck tires.

Goodyear found it could not expand the old plant in Dalian's Shahekou and will begin moving its production to a new plant in Pulandian by late 2010, when the construction is set to be finished.

The production transfer will be completed by 2012, when the Shahekou plant will be completely closed. "The factory will be Goodyear's most advanced, totally green factory. We have reduced the consumption of energy in our factory in Dalian by 20 percent," says Cohade.

The facility will focus on tires for cars, and also, for the first time in China, tires for buses and trucks. "That is an example of investing to build the future," says Cohade.

"In the meantime, for the next two years, we are going

GROWING
W I T H
CHINA
MNC EXECUTIVES
TALK ABOUT CHINA

116

to focus on the strategies that so far have led to positive results. Continuous improvements in costs, innovative products, building up the brand with the Goodyear Blimp, building up our distribution structure, and most importantly building the best team we can at Goodyear, because we have the best people, in the factory, in service, in marketing and in general administration," says Cohade.

By LI FANGFANG

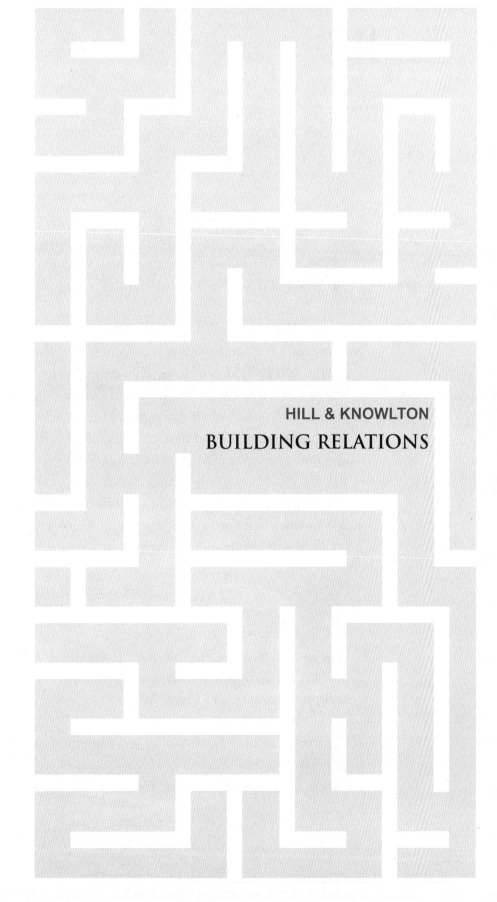

HILL & KNOWLTON
BUILDING RELATIONS

GROWING
W I T H
CHINA
MNC EXECUTIVES
TALK ABOUT CHINA

118

The idea of public relations began in China in 1984 when Hill & Knowlton spread the word.

Though the public relations (PR) industry is now regarded as one of the most promising sectors in China, the Chinese people had little idea of what PR was in the early 1980s, shortly after the nation's reform and opening-up began. They once associated PR (*gongguan* in Chinese) with relationship building around dining tables full of luxury dishes and liquor, and via expensive gifts and/or bribes.

Therefore, when US-headquartered Hill & Knowlton (H&K) launched the first PR agency in China in 1984, its courage won admiration as well as suspicion.

"When I heard the news that H&K would open a Beijing office, I was so proud," says James B. Heimowitz, who was then a media consultant for H&K Singapore and is now president and CEO, North Asia chairman of the PR agency. "My company had the ability to look forward and the willingness to invest in China before everybody else. I think that was a really smart move." At that time the market economy was only just emerging, while the planned economy was still holding sway and Chinese businesspeople hadn't realized the necessity of PR.

As a result, a priority for H&K then was to spread the concept of PR and tell the Chinese people what PR could achieve for them.

Fortunately for H&K, other foreign companies also entering into the Chinese market in the 1980s brought opportunities to the nascent Chinese PR industry.

They included electronic manufacturers from Japan, such as Panasonic, Sony and Toshiba, beverage giants Coca-Cola and PepsiCo as well as fast-food behemoths KFC and McDonald's from the United States. In order to establish corporate images and expand market shares, these companies needed PR agencies.

In 1984, an opening ceremony for IBM's first office in China was held in Beijing's Tian'anmen Square. The event was, of course, a milestone for IBM but also one for H&K as its first PR-generated event on the mainland.

Chinese businesses gradually realized the necessity of good PR, especially those that began taking their businesses and products overseas.

"We are trying to introduce international experience and expertise and marry them with Chinese enterprises and their own capabilities," says Heimowitz, a PR veteran with 25 years of experience.

In recent years, an increasing number of Chinese companies have been expanding into overseas markets or going public overseas. As a result, a pent-up need to build a good corporate image and better connect with

GROWING
W I T H
CHINA
MNC EXECUTIVES
TALK ABOUT CHINA

120

overseas investors, media and clients, has pushed Chinese companies to hire PR agencies.

"We have done more IPOs in China than anybody else," Heimowitz says with pride.

Baidu Inc., the biggest Chinese language search engine, launched its IPO on NASDAQ on August 5, 2005. Its stock price rose 353.85 percent on the first day of listing, making it the most successful company listed on NASDAQ since 2000. The PR agency serving Baidu was H&K.

In addition, PetroChina, Ping'an Insurance and China Construction Bank have all turned to H&K for IPO PR work.

"One of our proudest cases in China was our work with the Beijing Organizing Committee for the Games of the XXIX Olympiad (BOCOG)," Heimowitz says. The PR agency was appointed by BOCOG on April 27, 2006 as the only communications consultancy for the sports event.

According to Paul Taaffe, chairman and CEO of H&K, the company beat out seven other global agencies because of the H&K China team's commitment and dedication, the agency's knowledge of the Olympic movement and its large global network.

H&K helped both Athens and London win their bids for the summer Games and has been working for the International Olympic Committee for six years on strategic counsel and issues management.

Paul Taaffe (left), chairman and CEO of H&K, present at the signing ceremony on April 27, 2006 with the representatives of BOCOG, which hired H&K as the communications consultancy.

Founded in 1927, H&K, the member of the world's second largest communications group WPP Group, currently runs a global network of 71 offices in 41 countries and regions.

"So far, there is not only business coming into China, but also business going from China to the rest of the world," says Taaffe.

Following H&K, many other foreign PR companies stepped into the Chinese market and Chinese PR companies, such as Blue Focus, started up around 1995.

Competition is increasing with experienced foreigners vying for multinational clients and local counterparts engaging in price wars. But H&K says it is confident with its advantages.

H&K is a full service agency which covers 10 business sectors, including marketing, branding, investor relations,

GROWING
W I T H
CHINA
MNC EXECUTIVES
TALK ABOUT CHINA

122

digital communications, IT communications, public affairs, healthcare and pharmaceuticals, crisis and issues management, executive trainings, and media training.

H&K says the great challenge for not only itself but also the whole PR industry in China is finding experienced and talented personnel.

According to statistics from the Ministry of Labor and Social Security, demand for professional PR talents in China has risen 30 percent annually in recent years. But only one in a thousand in the mainland PR industry has received training in the field in college.

The demand is especially high given the rapid progress of China's PR industry. Statistics from China International Public Relations Association (CIPRA) show that the business volume of the Chinese PR industry exceeded 10.8 billion *yuan* in 2007, a 35 percent increase compared with the previous year.

"Many international companies want to double their size in China in the next three years and I am quite confident that PR will be in the center of their expansion strategy."

By TONG HAO

BREAKING GROUND

GROWING
W I T H
CHINA
MNC EXECUTIVES
TALK ABOUT CHINA
124

On February 21, 1972, when Richard Nixon stepped out of Air Force One to shake hands with Chinese Premier Zhou Enlai, the historical moment was witnessed by millions in the United States thanks to the live TV broadcasting.

Yet for Chinese engineers, what impressed them most were the Hewlett-Packard computers used for the satellite communications.

That was why the Chinese government immediately invited HP to send executives to Beijing to explore co-operation opportunities. But negotiations initially proved fruitless as most of the hi-tech gear China wanted to buy from HP was on a list of export goods banned by the US government when the Cold War still prevailed despite the thawing Sino-US relations.

However, it became a prelude to forming China's first hi-tech joint venture as well as HP's opportunity to begin riding on China's economic boom.

On January 1, 1979, China and the United States formally established diplomatic relations and when Deng Xiaoping met Henry Kissinger, the chief architect of China's economic reform eagerly asked Kissinger to recommend some US companies with which China could work to jumpstart the country's hi-tech sector.

Kissinger suggested HP and its co-founder David Packard visited Beijing in August and proposed a joint venture.

In fact, the US technology giant was already making preparations.

Early in June 1979, HP's chief operating officer Dean Morton already was urging Liu Jining, a Chinese engineer working at HP, to return to China to start up HP's China business.

Underlining HP executives' ambitious vision, Morton told Liu that "China is the world's only untapped market which promises unprecedented career opportunity", recalls Liu, who at that time was a bit reluctant to lead the mission.

Packard's visit proved a boon. During the discussions with Chinese State leaders and senior officials, he "highlighted the importance of the market as a driving force", says Liu. And "Packard said China's planned economy resulted in manufacturing products which were not needed by the market while there was a great inadequacy in manufacturing what the market really needed."

Packard told Chinese leaders that a market-oriented mechanism was necessary and that principle later became the cornerstone of HP's China business that integrates manufacturing, marketing and sales.

GROWING
WITH
CHINA
MNC EXECUTIVES
TALK ABOUT CHINA

126

"I believe that had some impact on Jiang Zemin's an-noucement to set building the socialist market economy as the goal of China's economic reform (at the 14th Na-tional Congress of Communist Party of China) in 1992 (which marked a departure from long years of planned economy)," Liu says.

In fact, the Deputy Minister of the Electronics and Indus-try and the vice-chairman of China National Electronics Import and Export Corporation (CEIEC) signed a Memo-randum of Understanding for forming HP's China joint venture during a visit to HP's headquarters in California and David Packard's home in June 1983.

Three months later, all of HP's board members flew to Beijing to hold its board meeting. That was a first for a US company although nowadays an increasing number of multinationals are doing so to highlight the impor-tance of the Chinese market.

In 1985, HP's joint venture was formally launched with the US company holding a 57.5 percent stake and CEIEC 27.5 percent. Two other Chinese companies took the remaining stake.

Liu became the first president of HP's China business, which was called China Hewlett-Packard Co. Ltd. The Chinese government granted the privilege to underline its eagerness to introduce advanced technologies from the United States. So far no other multinationals are allowed to use China as the first word in the names of their Chinese operations.

Riding on China Boom

HP's early entry into China as one of the world's biggest technology companies, gave a much-needed boost to China's economy as well as its drive to introduce foreign advanced technologies to revamp domestic industries.

The Commission of Science Technology and Industry for National Defense (COSTIND) oversaw the country's hi-tech industry for a long time. In the 1980s, COSTIND was the primary Chinese government body HP had to deal with, although these days much of its function has been transferred to the Ministry of Information Industry, Ministry of Science and Technology as well as the National Development and Reform Commission.

In 1981 HP won an order from the United Nations Development Program (UNDP) to provide China with five HP 3000 minicomputers. The US firm in fact developed the HP 3000 series in 1972 and released the products in 1973. However when they arrived in China even eight

Five HP 3000 microcomputers were delivered to the airport in Beijing in 1981. Authorities closed a street in the neighborhood just to unload the computers.

GROWING
W I T H
CHINA
MNC EXECUTIVES
TALK ABOUT CHINA

128

years later, it was still a big event in the country that was in dire need of advanced technologies.

Underlining the importance for China, when the HP 3000 minicomputers were delivered to the airport in Beijing in 1981, authorities closed a street in the neighborhood just to unload the computers. The Ministry of Foreign Trade and Economic Cooperation, which was the predecessor of the Ministry of Commerce, became the first user of HP computer products in China.

From 1985 to 1989, the first five years since the launch of China HP Co. Ltd., sales growth was sluggish. It hit US$40 million in 1989, up only from US$32 million in 1985. But the number of employees surged from 149 to 370 and it established two branches and four liaison offices, boding well for the firm that was ready to flex its muscles.

With China reforming its State-owned enterprises and multinationals swarming to the country, information technology spending in the country started to see a boom. And HP, which established a relationship with China much earlier than most of its peers, was quicker to capitalize on it.

In 1990 China HP netted annual revenue of US$74 million and increased it more than five fold to US$372 million in 1995. In 1999 the figure exceeded US$1 billion, making China HP the first joint venture in the country to see its yearly revenue hitting the billion US dollar benchmark.

Growing with China

After 2000 when Cheng-Yaw Sun became president of China HP, the firm took some unique approaches to expand its business as well as China's IT market. It launched the China HP Business School in 2001, which trained a lot of top-notch executives in the country. In 2002 it set up an IT management school as well as a software engineering institute in 2003. Inside China HP there is also a leadership development center with Sun as one of the lecturers.

"Only HP had so many training institutions. And for a time nearly half of the heads of top IT companies in China were trained at HP," says Sun. "Also the chiefs of many channel partners were influenced by HP's culture."

The policy enabled many Chinese companies to learn Western management practices, which boosted the domestic market although many eventually became HP's rivals such as Legend, now known as Lenovo, China's top PC maker.

Lenovo started its business by distributing IBM and HP's products in the 1980s. In fact, China HP's employee badge inspired the first one designed for Legend. "Yang Yuanqing learned all of the sales tactics from HP during 1994 and 1996, and after that he started to create his own pitches," Lin Yang, former vice-president of Digital China, was quoted by the *China Computer World* as saying.

Yang, who was a sales guru at Legend at that time, is now the helmsman of Lenovo that has already acquired IBM's PC-making business. And Digital China is a spin-off from Legend.

Although HP's training programs spawned many rivals which are posing a challenge to the US giant, Sun, who retired in 2007, believes that the move to China eventually benefited HP as the size of the whole market has expanded with the intensified competition.

Now the firm is ready to expand its market again by plugging into smaller cities and the rural market.

"In the first half of 2008, China HP plans to pene-trate into China's 600 fourth- and sixth-tier cities. That includes not only PCs, but also other products such as servers," says Foo Piau Phang, president of China HP.

By LI WEITAO

Leap of Faith

I had served at Hewlett-Packard for 25 years since I joined it in 1982. My work at China HP Co. Ltd. for 16 years gave me an opportunity to witness and participate in China's reform and opening-up process.

In 1991 I was assigned from HP Taiwan to China HP Co. Ltd. to oversee HP's computer business on the Chinese mainland. In 2000 I was appointed vice-president of HP's global operations as well as president of China HP Co. Ltd. and retired from these two posts in May 2007. I would like to describe the changes I witnessed during those 16 years in four aspects:

Cheng-Yaw Sun, President of China HP Co. Ltd. during 2000 to 2007

Dramatic change in the IT market

China's IT market, at its early stage, was subject to several constraining factors. The market was quite small as the government and businesses spent inadequate money on information technology infrastructure. The government had adopted an approval plan for imports of computers, while the United States and European countries were still practicing the Coordinating Committee for Multilateral Export Controls (CoCom), which put an embargo on Western exports to East Bloc countries including China.

Also a planned economy in China meant that the IT spending was mainly driven by the government's budget. All these factors limited the takeoff of China's IT market.

GROWING
W I T H
CHINA
MNC EXECUTIVES
TALK ABOUT CHINA

132

However, the market witnessed overwhelming changes when China was pushing forward its reform and opening-up policy. In 1994 the CoCom ceased to function.

The government's approval plan for computer imports was abridged, tariffs on IT products were dropped to zero and domestic firms started to revamp themselves in order to cope with a changing market environment.

The rapid rise of foreign investments and a slew of government policies to increase operating efficiency boosted an information technology swing in the country. The emergence and popularity of Internet, followed by the increasing income of the Chinese people, boosted consumer spending and turned the Chinese mainland into the most lucrative IT market in the world. That lured more global IT majors to invest in China and led to a rapid rise of many domestic companies.

On the second hand, major global IT players started to rethink their strategies in resource-rich China. Many companies started transferring manufacturing activities, research and development (R&D) and outsourcing to China. Now the country is the world's largest manufacturer of IT products and its strength in R&D and outsourcing is also on a sharp rise. More than 10 years ago I moved all of my family members to the Chinese mainland. Looking back, I never expected China's IT market would experience such dramatic changes. Neither did I expect China would have a crucial impact on the global IT market. China's reform and opening-up policy has affected every single industry in the country and all the people here. However, from a global perspective, I would say the policy impacted the IT market most.

Changes of customer demand

In the IT market, at its initial stage, major customers were the government agencies and the State-owned enterprises (SOEs). The private economy was quite small and limited almost only in Guangdong Province. As a result, customers' decisions in IT spending were constrained by bureaucratic practices, which always focused on doing things in a planned manner.

Thus, adopting the most advanced technologies, technology transfers and improving their own technological strength became the most important factors in affecting customers' decisions in choosing IT suppliers. But at the same time returns from investment, operating efficiency and cost cutting were largely ignored.

However, with the changes brought by the reform and opening-up policy, decision makers started to take costs, efficiency, return and speed into consideration.

They not only increased spending, but also changed their requirements for the IT divisions. IT divisions were no longer only units to provide technology support, but also operating units. Those experienced in business operations replaced the heads of IT divisions with technology backgrounds.

And the rapid development of the consumer market is challenging the ability of IT companies to respond to the fast-changing customer demands. Such changes have affected both customers and IT suppliers such as HP. We had to readjust our sales and service strategies in line with the market changes and customer demands. In fact, many IT companies, which entered China at an early time, have already been washed out of the market because they were unable to catch up with the changes.

GROWING
W I T H
CHINA
MNC EXECUTIVES
TALK ABOUT CHINA

134

China HP

China HP Co. Ltd. was established in 1985 and was the first Sino-US hi-tech joint venture. HP is one of the few global IT giants that are running their businesses in a joint venture manner in China. The establishment of China HP benefited from the improvement of Sino-US relations as well as the great importance Chinese government attached to the hi-tech sector. China HP used to focus mainly on sales and marketing, but in the past 23 years it has grown into a well-known hi-tech company that is now involved in various areas including manufacturing, R&D and outsourcing. Changes to both of its size and its importance to HP's global operations have been very dramatic.

Such an achievement could never be achieved without the effort from all of our employees, the support from our headquarters and customers and, most importantly, the support from Chinese government. Underlining that, HP was one of the very first IT companies allowed to conduct manufacturing, R&D and sales in China.

The most crucial factor to China HP's rapid growth is our ability to make constant changes to adapt to the market and customer demand. In 1991 when I joined China HP, I actually had an impression that I was joining a State-owned company. As it was a joint venture between HP and the Chinese government, many management practices were greatly influenced by government policies such as a ceiling on salaries, free dormitories, company shuttle buses, a rigid recruitment policy as well as various welfare policies. The way a State-owned enterprise is run overshadowed every part of China HP. That gave rise to confusion in our corporate culture. China HP's corporate culture was different from that in HP's operations elsewhere.

However, after Deng Xiaoping's inspection tour to South China in 1992, China HP's executives were determined to introduce a slew of reform policies to adapt market changes and rebuild China HP with a goal to become a globally competitive business.

China HP was one of the first to join Beijing municipality government's pilot in a housing policy. We amended the housing distribution policy and free company shuttle buses. Instead we provided employees loans to buy flats, sold the dormitories to employees, integrated welfare into the salaries and significantly increased salaries. We also changed many management practices such as the approval policy on employees' overseas trips, and abridged a system which required a dual-leadership from both Chinese and foreign parties as prescribed by the agreement when forming the joint venture.

HP's board also gave the president of China HP more empowerment. And we also conformed China HP's management practices to those of HP's operations elsewhere in the world. I would say China HP would not reform itself and would never attain its large achievements without the sound environment created by China's social and economic reforms.

Also, to capitalize on the market opportunities brought by the changes, China HP also introduced strategic reorganization by improving our service offerings, market coverage, building more subsidiaries, getting closer to the local market and customers, tailoring products to local markets, increasing investment and strengthening manufacturing, R&D, as well as outsourcing.

My own career

Joining China HP was a big decision not only for my own career development, but also for all of my family. When HP headquarters asked me of my willingness to work on the Chinese mainland in 1991, I said, "yes", within less than two minutes. Many people believed I was risking my career and did not understand why I would leave HP Taiwan, where I had a promising future. But years later, many people envied me as I made the decision much earlier than others to develop my career on the mainland and grasped the chance to grow with one of the most successful growth stories.

My experience on the mainland has been the most important and crucial chapter in my life. The booming mainland market broadened my career opportunities and enriched my experience, knowledge and skills. I have retired from China HP and relocated my family to the United States but my link with the mainland remains intact. That is also partly because my son is married to a mainland lady. I'm really grateful to HP, my former colleagues, customers, partners, the government and my friends, and most importantly, the reform and opening-up policy which has given me numerous opportunities.

(Cheng-Yaw Sun, the author of this article, is the former president of China HP Co. Ltd. during 2000 to 2007. His leadership helped HP earn a reputation as the most admired multinational in China for several consecutive years and himself as one of the most respected home-grown chief of a multinational's China operation.)

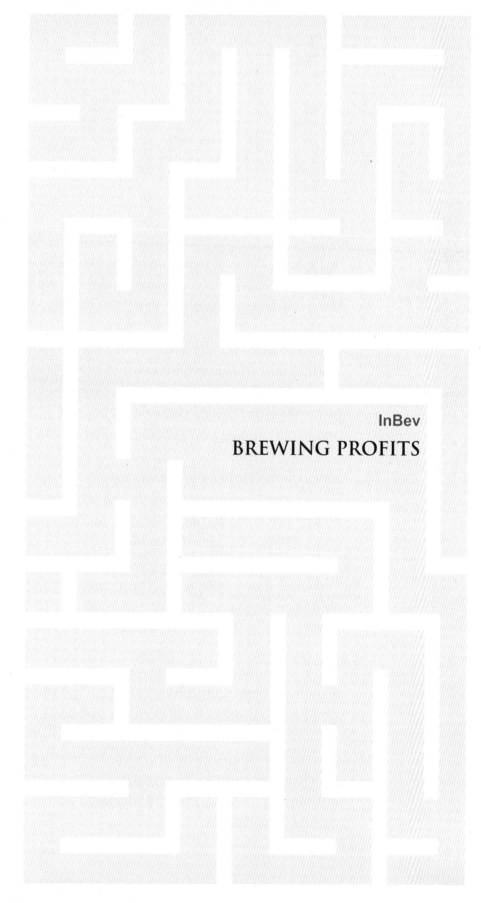

InBev
BREWING PROFITS

Miguel Patricio, president of the International brewer InBev Asia Pacific, plans to display the statue of Deng Xiaoping in his office in downtown Shanghai.

"Deng should be the most respected person in this world's fastest growing economy," says Patricio. "The prosperous and modern city outside this window should be credited to Deng's decision to begin the economic reform and opening-up policy in the late 1970s."

Although the Portuguese native paid his first visit to China late in 2007 and took over the helm from in January 2008, he has made Deng his idol since he got to know about China's changes during his middle school years.

"I should show more respect to Deng, because he created such a good economic environment for InBev to grow in this great brewing market."

The Leuven, Belgium-based beer maker was one of the first international companies to engage the Chinese market just after it opened the doors to the world.

In the early 1980s, Belgium Artois Engineering — from which InBev eventually originated — set up business in China by helping Zhujiang Brewery with technology transfer, says Patricio.

"InBev brings you the World of Beer" staged at Beer Festival attracted thousands of beer lovers.

At that time, the Chinese market was just opening-up to only a few with domestic breweries leading the pack.

In the late 1990s, Interbrew, a Belgium brewery that came as a result of a merger between Artois Engineering and another Belgium beer group, Piedboeuf, entered China when it bought Jinling Brewery in Nanjing. Interbrew later became InBev after a merger with the Brazil-based AmBev in 2004.

"Throughout the 1990s, the Chinese market was very fragmented with many small local players and small local brands. Some of the global brewers entered the Chinese market to promote global brands, but most of them failed or withdrew from the market," says Patricio.

InBev's current global rival Denmark-based Carlsberg, one of the top five brewers in the world, entered China

GROWING
W I T H
CHINA
MNC EXECUTIVES
TALK ABOUT CHINA

140

in 1978. It invested US$80 million to establish a joint venture in Shanghai with Tsingtao Brewery in 1997, producing its own beer in an effort to get a large share of China's high-end beer market.

However, two years later, Carlsberg's market share in China was only 1.82 percent. Carlsberg encountered a loss of 170 million *yuan* and had to sell its 75 percent of share in the venture to Tsingtao Brewery by 150 million *yuan* in 2000.

Interbrew also changed its strategy in China. "We realized that we had to be local and closer to the customer and pay more attention to the preponderant and potential regional brands, other than building a national brand in such a big and sophisticated market."

Later in 2002, Interbrew spent 160 million *yuan* on a 24 percent of stake in Zhujiang Brewery — one of the Chinese industry leaders, in Guangdong Province, and in 2003, it acquired a 70 percent of share in KK Brewery in Zhejiang Province.

And by purchasing Lion Group Brewery interests in 2004, "which gave us scale of operation, we became the foreign shareholder of Lion's 12 breweries in China," says Patricio.

In 2005, Interbrew acquired Dangyang Snow Leopard Brewery in Yichang, Hubei Province to set up its wholly-owned enterprise.

Its 5.8-billion-*yuan* 100 percent purchase of Sedrin Brewery in Fujian Province in 2006 was recorded in China's brewing industry as the biggest takeover by revenue. "It doubled our size in China," says Patricio. InBev has invested more than 1.2 billion euros in China over the past two decades.

"This investment indeed signifies InBev's commitment to China. We are very optimistic about the business opportunities in China. We are making further investment in technical renovation and introducing global best practices to the day-to-day management of our breweries in China," says Patricio.

Today, InBev China runs or jointly runs 33 breweries across eight provinces — Fujian, Guangdong, Hubei, Hunan, Jiangsu, Jiangxi, Zhejiang and Hebei — and employs almost 22,000 people.

It has been active in the beer market in southeast China while the northern market is firmly controlled by Beijing-based China Resources Snow Breweries, China's No. 1 brewery with annual production capacity of 6.9 million kl.

In July 2008, US brewer Anheuser-Busch accepted a US$52 billion takeover bid from InBev, creating the world's largest beer maker AB-InBev that will produce a quarter of the world's beer. "We are excited about the opportunities and prospects brought by the InBev-AB merger, around the world and in China," says Patricio.

After the deal, InBev will obtain AB's 27 percent stake in China's Tsingtao, the leading Chinese premium brewer, as well as ownership of the Harbin Brewery Group's 13 breweries.

"We respect and honor the strategic partnership forged between AB and Tsingtao. More importantly, we respect Tsingtao as China's national brand and international brand and have every intention to build a creative and productive partnership with Tsingtao for future," says Patricio.

"By doing so, we hope to create more opportunities for the Chinese beer market and bring more choice to the Chinese consumers in the future."

In addition, AB-InBev will own AB's Budweiser, which is a growing brand in China and Corona Extra, which is the No. 5 brand globally. AB-InBev's China business will definitely be enhanced by AB's strength in northeastern China.

"China will always be our key strategic market in the world because it's the world's largest and fastest growing beer market by volume," says Patricio.

"For example, volume will increase 62 percent in next 10 years in China. In comparison, US volume growth is at 5.8 percent," he adds.

China's beer drinking per capita was 26.4 liters in 2006. In comparison, the Czech Republic, which ranks No. 1 worldwide, was 160 liters per capita in 2006.

"As China's economy develops, more and more consumers will drink beer. And the per capita consumption will hopefully increase as well," says Patricio. "All these provide a very positive environment for beer manufacturers, including AB-InBev, to develop in China in the next decade."

Cheers to China!

Miguel Patricio experienced a memorable trip during his first visit to China in 2007. He flew from Canada to Beijing, then to Fuzhou, and took a car to Putian, more than 100 km south of Fuzhou, to visit InBev's brewery there. He was struck by the huge differences between China's cities and rural regions.

Miguel Patricio, President of InBev Asia Pacific

But with years of experiences living and working for InBev in seven countries from Europe, South America, and North America to Asia, Patricio is confident about his career in this dynamic country and believes the potential market will provide InBev with a brighter future. In a recent exclusive interview in his new office in Shanghai, Patricio shared his views.

Q: What's the biggest challenge for your company in the Chinese market?

A: As a foreign player in China, we have to deal with historical outstanding issues such as shareholders, people and land, when we want to restructure and integrate our operations in China.

Secondly, competition in China is getting fiercer in recent years. Some of the players have irrational behavior and fight price wars. Just like everyone else, we need to constantly balance profitability with volume growth. Moreover, over the past year, we see the price increases of raw materials going through the roof.

GROWING
W I T H
CHINA
MNC EXECUTIVES
TALK ABOUT CHINA
144

However, by insisting on our strategy of a winning brand portfolio, winning at the point of connection, enhancing world-class brewing efficiency and targeting external growth, we believe our dream — the best beer company in a better world, our people, and our culture will drive our success in China.

Q: **What are your company's contributions to China's brewery industry?**

A: When InBev entered the Chinese market in 1984 we transferred brewing technology and management knowhow to Zhujiang Brewery in Guangzhou. This commitment to working with our partners has been the foundation of our approach ever since.

Since then, we have built a number of partnerships in China. In each of these we have worked with our partners to share our knowledge and experience in the industry.

We remain steadfastly committed to building partnerships with Chinese breweries. We believe this approach supports the adoption of global best practices across the industry — including management, procurement, marketing, sales, distribution, and environmentally responsible brewing.

In addition, our business continues to help support the local economies in which we operate, from investment in new breweries to employment and generating tax for local governments. In the last financial year we contributed approximately 1.3 billion *yuan* in tax revenue to local government.

Q: Nowadays, the environment and energy crisis has become a global issue. As an energy consuming manufacturer, what efforts have you made for a better world?

A: InBev is a global leader in promoting environmentally friendly brewing processes through water and energy conservation, as well as recyclable and environmentally friendly packaging.

For example, our two new breweries in Zhoushan of Zhejiang Province and Changsha of Hunan Province, are fitted with modern and efficient technologies, enabling us to put China on the map to implement global environmental best practices. In the Zhoushan Brewery, InBev's filtration technology will for the first time be applied. The technology only uses regenerable filtration aids and will save 90 tons of waste in Zhoushan. Moreover, we have saved 60,000 tons of coal equivalent and seven millions tons of water in the past three years.

Q: As president of a multinational company's operation in Asia-Pacific and based in China, what's your view of China's 30 years of reform and opening-up?

A: China today plays a significant role on the world's stage. The just completed Beijing Olympics is a demonstration of China's importance and contribution to the world. The prosperity of China today shows that 30 years ago Chinese leader Deng Xiaoping made the most significant and wise decision for China and its people. For InBev, as the world's largest brewer, we had the opportunity to do business in China as a result of Deng's open-door policy. We believe we can make a difference here by providing quality beer choices to Chinese consumers.

Q: What are your expectations for China?

A: We are optimistic about the prospect of developing our business in China. We have received much support from local governments. We look forward to continued support from the central government for our business development. We are very glad to see that over the years, law and regulations have been more clearly defined, which definitely help us in making investment decisions.

Q: What's your ambition in the Chinese market?

A: Compared to the leading Chinese brands, Tsingtao, Snow and Yanjing, we are still relatively small and new to China. We respect our Chinese competitors and have a lot to learn from them. Currently, we are running a brand portfolio of seven Chinese local brands. Our goal is to integrate our business across the 20-some breweries and implement global best practices to increase the efficiency of the operations.

InBev's global mission is to build the best beer company in a better world. We promote responsible drinking to consumers and good environmental performance in our breweries. We are committed to building a Chinese national brand and upgrading regional brands. We will continue to improve the standard of China's beer industry by working together with Chinese partners. I am full of optimism for the beer industry and InBev's development in China.

By LI FANGFANG

ROOM WITH A VIEW

GROWING
W I T H
CHINA
MNC EXECUTIVES
TALK ABOUT CHINA

148

There is probably no better word than "exciting" to sum up how Bill Marriott felt about his most recent visit to China in September 2007.

The 76-year-old chairman and CEO of Marriott International (Marriott), a global lodging company with a history as long as 81 years, is also the son of J. Willard Marriott, the company's founder.

Marriot visited China especially to celebrate the completion of Marriott's 3,000th hotel, the 588-room JW Marriott Hotel Beijing in the capital's newest luxury property complex — China Central Place — which opened in November 2007.

"I have been very impressed by the city's drive, energy and focus as it prepares for the Olympic Games. We are thrilled to be part of these exciting times for China and Beijing, and look forward to doing our part to offer a historic and memorable experience for all of our guests," said Marriott during his speech at the ceremony.

There is little doubt that nearly 20 years ago, when Marriott made its first foray into the nation, the group's chairman would never have expected that firstly such a remarkable event would happen in China and secondly

China would and will continue to have such a significant role in the company's corporate development strategy.

Back in 1927, J. Willard Marriott and his partner Hugh Colton opened their A&W root beer stand in Washington. In 1957 the business expanded into a lodging portfolio when the motor hotel — Twin Bridges — opened in Virginia, signaling the beginning of the group's hotel business.

For many years, "the corporate's focus was on North America, due to the opportunities for growth in the United States," says Geoff Garside, executive vice-president of Marriott Asia-Pacific, who joined Marriott in 1977 and is now in charge of business in Asia and Australia.

"It was not until the 1980s that we began to look at it internationally." And the first destination abroad was China. In 1989, Marriott opened its first Chinese hotel, JW Marriott Hotel Hong Kong, which was also its first hotel in Asia.

Garside was then transferred from general manager (GM) of JW Marriott Hotel in Los Angeles to GM of the first China hotel, and his career has since been closely connected to the world's most populous nation and fastest growing economy.

What attracted Marriott to HK at that time was "the cheap labor costs", but the reason Marriott did not choose Chinese mainland to invest in, which has a lower labor cost than Hong Kong, lied in the immaturity of the local hospitality market.

Courtyard Beijing.

Mainland Business

Since 1978 HK-based Peninsula Hotels moved to the
mainland. In April 1982 Beijing Jian'guo Hotel, the first
foreign hotel group entered the mainland market. The
company was followed by other international groups.
However, the local hospitality industry during the 1980s
and the early 1990s was still in its infancy as a result of
the slackened tourism market.

It was Hong Kong, especially in the 1990s, that set quality
standard for the global hotel business. Usually "many
executives from the US and Europe quickly flew back to
HK and stay there after having handling business in the
mainland," Garside recalls.

JW Marriott Hotel Hong Kong has a unique policy.

It was the only one of its kind to conduct a two-day-off system for all associates, not only for managers, and was also one of the few that provided the associates a non-hierarchy environment where they could call one other, and even their bosses, by their first names, and encouraged them to make decisions on how to best serve guests.

It was not until 1995 that Marriott decided to crack the mainland market by opening Shenyang Marriott Hotel in northeast China's Liaoning Province, the first five-star hotel in the provincial capital.

Two years later, it signed a package of hotel properties, seven in total, including Courtyard by Marriott Beijing, Courtyard by Marriott Shunde and China Marriott Hotel, Guangzhou.

Stimulated by the stronger local economy and the booming tourism market, in the past 13 years, Marriott's portfolio in China has grown quickly, covering more than 30 hotels offering 11,547 rooms representing its six major brands.

And the group's local expansion strategy has been consistent, setting sight on "the gateway cities", says Garside.

Marriott Executive Apartments Palm Springs Beijing.

GROWING
W I T H
CHINA
MNC EXECUTIVES
TALK ABOUT CHINA

152

China is becoming a strategically significant market for Marriott since its entry into the World Trade Organization in 2001.

During the past few years, China has "held the first position around Asia by contributing more than 40 percent of Asian sales revenue for Marriott".

And the momentum is set to continue. In the next three years, "there will be an additional 100 hotels in Asia coming out, 40 percent of which will be located in China," says Garside.

"And the other 40 percent will be in India, and the rest goes to the other parts of Asia. China and India will be the largest two."

QUAN Spa Garden.

Talent-oriented Strategy

An undeniable truth is that Marriot was slow in entering the Chinese mainland, about 17 years after the first international hospitality brand entered the local market.

Besides the Peninsula, in the 1980s, some, if not many, international hotel groups had successively shown up.

Following the Peninsula were the United Kingdom-based International Hotels Group (IHG) and HK-based Shangri-La in 1984, French Accor and the US-based Sheraton in 1985 and the Hilton in 1988.

Nowadays Marriott's expansion rate is not striking either. IHG says it will open 125 hotels in China by 2008; Accor plans to obtain a portfolio of 180 properties around China by 2010.

But these do not cast any shadow on the fairly high brand's awareness and recognition among the local guests, which Marriott's hotel business in China is heavily relying on.

"The occupancy rate of Marriott hotels in China averages 70 to 80 percent," says Garside.

Site is one of the key concerns for the group and Marriott seems very careful in choosing properties.

The exterior appearances of almost all Marriott hotel buildings are nothing short of eye-catching. Besides the newly established twin hotels in China Central Place,

GROWING
W I T H
CHINA
MNC EXECUTIVES
TALK ABOUT CHINA
154

the JW Marriott Hotel Beijing and the 305-room Ritz-Carlton Beijing, the 369-room JW Marriott Hotel Shanghai, which opened in 2003, is located in the city's most bustling commercial district, Nanjing Road, and has won many awards for its design; China Marriott Hotel in Guangzhou is one of the first slew of five-star hotels in the southern city, settling down opposite the major exhibition hall of the bi-annual Canton Fair.

But the more impressive side of Marriott is its quality service, a more important factor in the operation of hotel businesses.

The Ritz-Carlton Hotel, the most luxury hotel brand worldwide acquired by Marriott in 1998, sets a shining example in the global industry for the service motto it claims — "We are ladies and gentlemen serving ladies and gentlemen."

The Portman Ritz-Carlton Shanghai has won the reward of "the Best Employer in Asia" from Hewitt Associates, a global consulting company, for three consecutive years since 2001.

Marriott itself has also been keen in "paying attention to details" since the first day of its business. That "success is never final" was an expression its founder had been fond of.

Talents are the driving force behind its success. J. Willard Marriott frequently said, "people — their development, loyalty, interest and team spirit — are No. 1."

There are over 20 different training programs for managers and associates to choose from for outstanding hotel performance and personal growth.

Marriott is one of the few hotel management companies that require hotels to contribute a minimum of US$750 a year in professional development for all managers. In addition, 15 minutes per day is committed to training all associates per management contract of the property.

"We are lucky as there are only two chairmen in Marriott's history, and they share the same philosophy (on management)," says Garside.

To make sure its philosophy is well conducted around China, Marriott is very selective in choosing partners. And the most required principle in the negotiation is that they "share similar philosophy — developing and training associates and managers and getting them locally," says Garside.

It always plays a significant role in the hotel business whether the hotel group and the owner could share the same philosophy. Hilton, the famous American hotel group has tasted the bitterness for failing in reaching consensus on talent development with the owners, insiders say. It has opened only five hotels in China while its business partners have changed substantially in the mean time.

More the Marriott

The start of China's reform and opening-up policy in 1978 marked the beginning of the nation's hospitality industry.

In the past three decades, especially in the past eight years, a number of international hotel groups have piled into the Chinese mainland to cash in on the booming economy.

In many ways Marriott International does not seem like a standout company in China. It was not the first to enter into the mainland and it's not the fastest growing hotel group there, either.

But the outlook and culture of the American company, with an 80-year history, and its commitment to winning over guests and keeping them loyal, has created a good impression on many Chinese people's mind.

In an exclusive interview in June 2008, Geoff Garside, executive vice-president of Marriott Asia-Pacific, talked about his views on the company's China development in the past and the future.

Q: You were appointed to work in Hong Kong in 1989 when Marriott first entered China, and you have seen Marriott's track record in China. How many different phases has Marriott experienced since?

A: It's hard to break them up. 1997 was a catalyst year when Marriott purchased Renaissance in China. This brought us more exposure both to travelers and to ho-

Geoff Garside,
Executive vice-president of
Marriott Asia-Pacific

tel owners. Another catalyst was the completion of JW Marriott Hotel Shanghai opening in 2003, as it was of very high quality in many aspects and very visible. In the past seven years, our China business has done especially well.

There are some criteria we use when we enter a new market. We look at gateway cities first and we look for long-term partnership for five years at least, and then we look for partners that understand our philosophy.

Q: Has there been any difficult patches for Marriott China over the last two decades?

A: Not really, there were business downturns in China such as during the SARS epidemic, but that affected everybody including Marriott.

The hotel business is not easy. There are always challenges, such as constant learning, learning about new cities, new hotels, new locations, and new owners.

GROWING
W I T H
CHINA
MNC EXECUTIVES
TALK ABOUT CHINA
158

Above all probably finding and developing enough people is the most challenging thing. Hospitality is a labour intense business.

Anyway at Marriott there is always hope for everybody. I started working in the kitchen, and there are many examples in which people have developed.

Q: What makes Marriott different from others in the industry?

A: What distinguishes us is developing people. There is a statement from the corporate founder, saying "take good care of the associates and they'll take good care of

JW Marriott Hotel
Hong Kong.

the customers and they'll return again and again." Many companies talk about it (developing people) a lot, but I am afraid they can't always follow through with the philosophy.

Q: You mentioned that China and India would be the next two key areas for the company. What is the difference between the two in the hotel market?

A: There are several big differences. China is quicker in building hotels. It usually takes two years to see a property erected; but in India, it takes more than three years.

Infrastructure in China is better, so is the traffic. And the Chinese are willing to learn and be trained. Business is easier in China. But the only thing that is difficult in China is that we spend a lot more efforts teaching English. It is not necessary in India. But it is not a problem. We just need time to improve this.

Q: What effect do you think the Beijing Olympic Games will have on the local hotel industry?

A: The year 2008 will be a solid year. Obviously, the hotel business would be very busy during the Olympics. And it is also the same after the games, as more leisure and business travelers will want to visit China then to see what is happening here. We will see a spill-over later in 2008.

By the opening of the 2008 Olympics, Marriott expects to operate 11 hotels in Beijing to help accommodate the two million visitors expected to visit the city.

GROWING
W I T H
CHINA
MNC EXECUTIVES
TALK ABOUT CHINA

160

Q: What will be Marriott's next step in China?

A: I think Marriott's business will continue to grow in the next 10 years. The second- and third-tier cities will be the next focus. Courtyard (a moderate-tier brand) will be more important than the others and will be the next opportunity for Marriott, as the brand appeals to the domestic customers, especially the middle managers.

Q: What is your biggest concern?

A: Being able to grow and develop talents in China.

By DING QINGFEN

McDonald's

MC GROWING

GROWING
W I T H
CHINA
MNC EXECUTIVES
TALK ABOUT CHINA
162

Jim Skinner,
Vice-chairman and
CEO of McDonald's

During the Olympic month, when eating in McDonald's, you could hear the song, "China wins, we win", broadcast repeatedly.

Jim Skinner, vice-chairman and CEO of the world's largest fast-food company, says he appreciates the slogan.

Actually, he has reason to mean what he says. Since setting up the first McDonald's in China in Shenzhen in 1990, the Western restaurant chain has been expanding steadily and successfully. So far, other than the home market — the United States — China is the No. 1 growth market for McDonald's, with 960 restaurants and over 60,000 employees.

For 2008, China represents one third of all capital expenditures in the Asia-Pacific, Middle East and Africa region, where the fast-food giant is in 37 markets, according to Skinner.

"We've been steadily growing with China for the past 18 years and are very excited for what the future holds," he says.

In October 1990, the leading global fast food chain chose Shenzhen, a pioneer Special Economic Zone in

Guangdong Province bordering Hong Kong, to open its first 500-seat store in the developing market. Located on Jiefang Road, Shenzhen's busiest commercial area, McDonald's quickly won over the local consumers with its Ronald McDonald clown, Golden Arches or the yellow M logo, and Big Mac.

However, McDonald's was not the first fast-food chain on the mainland. In November 1987, the US-headquartered KFC launched its first China outlet in Qianmen of Beijing, an area neighboring Tian'anmen Square.

KFC's great success during a short period of time spurred McDonald's to China, a country that embraced the reform and opening-up policy in 1978, when Chinese curiosity about the West was at a peak. It was really a bold idea at that time, because China is a nation that takes pride in the delicacy and diversity of its cuisine which dates back to thousands of years ago, critics say.

In addition, while the monthly salary of urban residents in key cities at that time was 120 to 130 *yuan*, a 10 *yuan* Big Mac and double-cheeseburger at 5 *yuan* were not affordable for most.

But many Chinese still flocked to the store, due to its many attractions. Except for the delicious burgers, crispy French fries and icy milk shakes, there was the image of an affable and farcical Ronald McDonald, the striking yellow, red and blue decor, the smiling attendants and the quick service, in sharp contrast to the poor service consumers had long endured at local restaurants.

GROWING
W I T H
CHINA
MNC EXECUTIVES
TALK ABOUT CHINA

164

The success of the Shenzhen outlet prompted McDonald's to expand its chain nationwide. The then largest restaurant in terms of area for the fast-food behemoth was opened in 1992 at Beijing Wangfujing Street, the bustling commercial street of the capital city.

By the first quarter of 2002, there were 460 McDonald's outlets around China. The figure reached 600 at the end of 2004. At the same time, its arch rival in China KFC expanded its network to 1,200.

So far, KFC has around 2,200 stores dotted around China's 465 cities. It is expanding at the rate of one store a day, reaching further into the counties, while McDonald's plans to have 1,000 stores in China by the end of 2008. But McDonald's indicates it pays more attention to "same-restaurant performance".

"We have a business model of getting better versus getting bigger. It's not about how many restaurants you have, it's about how many restaurants that serve your customers well. It's not about how big, it's about how good and how you run your business," says Jeffrey Schwartz, McDonald's China CEO.

In early August 2008, McDonald's reported an eight percent increase in July global same-store sales, and its Asia-Pacific, Middle East and Africa region saw 7.2 percent growth, driven by extended hours and menu varieties, especially in Australia and China.

However, despite Schwartz's note of "getting better versus getting bigger", McDonald's has not stopped ag-

Jeff Schwartz,
McDonald's China
CEO and McDonald's
Olympic Champion
Crew team cheering
"i'm lovin' China
Win!" at the opening
ceremony of the
Official Restaurant of
the Olympic Games.

gressively increasing the number of its outlets in China. The company will open 125 restaurants in 2008, 150 in 2009 and 175 in 2010 across the country, says McDonald's CEO Skinner.

Compared with that in 1990, McDonald's menu in China has grown and includes foods tweaked for local tastes to satisfy consumers.

But Schwartz says that the hamburger and fries Western style is still at the heart of the Chinese menus.

"We do extensive focus group studies of Chinese consumers, and one of the things that Chinese consumers say over and over again is that 'we come to you because you are a Western brand, if we want rice or congee we can eat at home or in Chinese restaurants, we want to sample the Western brand,'" he says.

Some of the menu ideas developed in China have been exported to other markets around the world. Take corn cup as an example, it was invented by the McDonald's China Research and Development Center and proved to be very popular due to its healthy content and flavor and it has been introduced to other Asian marketplaces.

Skinner visited China in August for the Beijing 2008 Olympic Games, as McDonald's was an official partner of the event.

"We are very proud to be here," says the global CEO.

The mainland's fast-food market was worth almost US$200 billion in 2007 and was growing 16 percent per year, sources from the Ministry of Commerce say.

"We are going to continue our growth at a faster rate in China, while it has little to do with the association with Olympics, China is a huge market with great opportunities for businesses around the world, and it's no different for McDonald's," he adds.

By LIU JIE

Mercedes-Benz

BIG BENZ

China's first "one-child" generation is literally the driving force behind the country's thriving auto market, but in the early 1980s, most of their parents were still striving for a *Feige* (Flying Pigeon) bicycle as the ultimate in personal transportation.

"At that time, owning a bicycle was still a luxury for Chinese. With a salary of less than 50 *yuan* per month, nobody dared to dream of someday owning cars cost-

A new S-Class
Mercedes-Benz sedan
runs in Beijing.

ing hundreds of thousands *yuan*," says a Mercedes-Benz owner who purchased an E-Class sedan in 2005.

It was in the 1990s, when few nouveau riche began driving their private cars that some Chinese businessmen began to yearn for a "*Daben*" (big Benz), the Chinese nickname for Mercedes-Benz.

However, in the new century owning a Mercedes-Benz is becoming a reality rather than a dream for China's new generation.

Recently, the German luxury automaker officially launched its locally produced C-Class sedans priced between 378,000 and 478,000 *yuan*, targeting younger, newly affluent Chinese.

In the first quarter of 2008, Mercedes-Benz sold 9,626 luxury sedans in China, a 40 percent increase year-on-year, which is a sales figure the company never imagined when it entered the Chinese market.

"In the history of the world, no country has changed as much as China has in the past 30 years, and it is amazing not only to watch it, but to be a part of it and help contribute to it," says Ulrich Walker, chairman and CEO of Daimler Northeast Asia Ltd., parent of Mercedes-Benz (China) Ltd.

Actually, Mercedes-Benz was selling vehicles in China in 1913, when it had a sales office in Qingdao, Shandong Province, which was then a major German business and military enclave in China.

GROWING
W I T H
CHINA
MNC EXECUTIVES
TALK ABOUT CHINA
170

"Since then, we've been importing vehicles to China in varying capacities, but now we are proud to produce the Mercedes-Benz C- and E-Class vehicles here," says Walker.

In 1980, just one year after the Chinese government permitted ownership of private automobiles, the company set up a Daimler-Benz liaison office in Beijing in anticipation of the potential of the Chinese market for luxury sedans. It was the first such supplier in China.

But the Benz brand was still unknown in China, which was a slight irony given that Karl Benz created the first modern gasoline-powered automobile (the Motorwagen) in 1885.

So "in 1986, we established Mercedes-Benz China in Hong Kong, mainly because the economy there was already quite developed," says Walker.

In the late 1980s, Mercedes-Benz's flagship models 250S and 280SEL replaced the Hongqi (Red Flag) sedan as the official cars for a few high-level Chinese leaders, but it was still unknown to the general public.

As the Chinese mainland became increasingly open to the outside world, more consumers began to realize that the three-pointed star logo stood for wealth and prestige and they began to be crazy for the brand.

By 2000, the total automobile production in China had increased rapidly from 220,000 units in 1980 to 1.83 million units, making China the ninth biggest country in terms of auto production.

"We see great potential in the Chinese mainland with the growth of the luxury car market, a quickly growing economy, and a dramatic rise in the demand for luxury vehicles," says Klaus Maier, president and CEO of Mercedes-Benz (China) Ltd.

"With this thought in mind, we brought the S-Class to China first, following a strategy of logistics and service first, paving the way for more products to follow. Mercedes-Benz's business then healthily develops in the Chinese market," says Maier.

In 1993 and 1994, China's luxury sedan market enjoyed a short-lived boom when the government allowed foreign enterprises or joint ventures to buy duty-free imported vehicles in order to encourage more foreign investments.

By saving more than 100 percent of the tariffs, Mercedes-Benz became a hot ticket in 1994 with estimated sales of over 10,000 units that year.

However, in 1995, Mercedes-Benz's global rival, Volkswagen made the decision to produce its luxury sedan Audi in a joint venture with China FAW Group Corp in Changchun, Jilin Province. And in 1996, the first Audi 200 V6 rolled off the production line.

With Audi's star model A6's coming into the market in 1999, the local-produced sedan with competitive price soon won the luxury market with sales of 6,911 units that year.

Mercede-Benz's other major German competitor, BMW,

In November 2006,
Beijing Automotive
Industry Holding Co.
Ltd. chairman Xu Heyi
(right) held hands with
Daimler CEO Dieter
Zetsche (center)
and Ulrich Walker,
chairman and CEO
of Daimler Northeast
Asia Ltd., to celebrate
the inauguration of the
new plant under their
joint venture Beijing
Benz-DaimlerChrysler
Automotive Co. Ltd.

also formed a joint venture with Chinese Brilliance Auto in 2003 to begin producing BMW limousines in Shenyang, Liaoning Province.

In 1984, Mercedes-Benz talked to FAW in hopes that the Chinese company could use Mercedes-Benz's technology to retool its homegrown luxury Hongqi sedan. However, that plan was aborted in 1986 for unknown reasons.

It wasn't until 2005 that Mercedes-Benz finally established a joint venture, Beijing Benz-Daimler Chrysler Automotive (BBDC), with Beijing Automotive Industry Holding Co. (BAIC), and started producing E-Class autos.

"Daimler Northeast Asia and Mercedes-Benz have a long-term commitment to China. We are very happy to have great partners in China, and we are working together to introduce new vehicle technology and manufacturing technology to China," says Walker.

Moreover, "in 2006 we cemented our long-term commitment to China with Mercedes-Benz China Ltd. moving from Hong Kong to Beijing," adds Walker.

In 2007, Mercedes-Benz began producing MB Vito/Viano and Sprinter vehicles together with partners of Fujian Motors Group and Taiwan-based China Motors Corp.

"And early in 2008, we saw the all-new locally produced C-Class hit the market, expanding our local presence and deepening our relationship with BBDC," Maier adds.

J.D. Power & Associates forecasts luxury auto sales in China will more than double by 2014, to around 508,000.

"To continue to be automotive pioneers, we have to bring our latest technology to China in the shortest time possible. We are bringing more of our lineup to China,

Mercedes-Benz will introduce its smart mini car brand to the Chinese market in 2009.

investing in capacity, hiring more people and looking at increasing R&D and design in China as well," says Walker.

Dozens of premium models including the imported passenger car, sports car, and SUVs as well as locally produced C-Class and E-Class have been launched in China and have become best-sellers in their market segments. Mercedes also introduced the extremely high-end AMG brand to China in 2007 and sold 300 units in nine months, an amount "far greater than our original expectations," says Maier.

"We continue learning that in order to be successful here, one must localize," says Maier. "As a global company, we must find the right balance between international standards and local practices. In addition to producing the C- and E-Class vehicles in Beijing, we will continue localizing our operations, our supply chain and our people."

"China is very significant for Mercedes-Benz and Daimler AG. As one of the fastest growing markets in the world, we place great emphasis on our long-term commitment. As mentioned, we are producing more vehicles including vans here and sourcing more and more parts in China — for production in China, and for export," Walker adds.

At the Auto China 2008 Expo on April 20 in Beijing, "we brought more than 30 models for exhibition, including a global premiere which showed our focus on the Chinese market," says Maier.

Klaus Maier,
President and CEO
of Mercedes-Benz
(China) Ltd.

Ulrich Walker,
Chairman and CEO
of Daimler Northeast
Asia Ltd.

High Hopes

Ulrich Walker, chairman and CEO of Daimler North-east Asia Ltd. since November 2006, and Klaus Maier, president and CEO of Mercedes-Benz (China) Ltd. since January 2007, are two executives from Daimler-Benz's headquarters in Stuttgart, Germany, with notable achievements and experiences in the Asia-Pacific region. They live in Beijing, shouldering the challenging task of boosting the development of the company's Chinese branch and competing for the country's top spot in the high-end auto market. In an exclusive interview, Walker and Maier talked to reporter about the company's development and their expectations for the future.

Q: What's the biggest challenge for your company in China?

M: Our challenges in China are to continue providing world-class vehicles and service to our customers, and to continue to exceed the expectations of our customers.

GROWING
W I T H
CHINA
MNC EXECUTIVES
TALK ABOUT CHINA

176

With more and more capacity and competition, and with very sophisticated Chinese consumers, we have to continue to try and improve our service every day. Even though the three-pointed star has incredible brand value and many people dream of owning one, we can't rest on our laurels.

Q: **What's your future development plan to better serve the Chinese market?**

W: We want to bring more of our vehicles to China. And we want to build more vehicles including vans in China.

With local production it comes the need to localize our operations. We have a tremendous commitment to bring more China-based suppliers into our supply chain. Since we are still ramping up production, it has been challenging for suppliers to build their operations to meet our volume and quality targets in a short time. But we are committed to this at the highest levels of the company. We are working very aggressively to source more parts in China for production here as well as for global production.

Q: **Regarding Mercedes-Benz's development in China, are there any differences between that in this booming market and the ones in other countries, especially in Western countries?**

M: China is unique for its growth rate that is phenomenal. However, with more and more capacity, it gets more competition and more pressure on margins. This is similar in other parts of the world, but the long-term growth potential of China is unique. We have been pleased to see the growing awareness and willingness to finance vehicles in China. This has long been a practice in many Western countries, but it's still relatively new in China.

However, with creative financing and good rates, our financial services arm, DaimlerChrysler Auto Finance China, is making it easier for people to realize their dreams of owning a Mercedes-Benz.

Moreover, because of China's unique market circumstances, we've specially tailored certain models, such as the S300 and R300, to better meet the demands of Chinese customers.

Q: As presidents of a multinational company's operations in China and Northeast Asia, what are your views on China's 30 years of reform and opening-up?

W: Deng Xiaoping was one of the world's great leaders who had an instinctive knowledge of how to promote a successful environment for businesses. His experiments with special economic zones proved more successful than people even imagined.

Thanks to the principles laid down in the reform and opening-up policy, China is enjoying economic success that few could have imagined 30 years ago.

In 2008 when China hosted the Olympics, the world witnessed the incredible progress and development of China. Companies like ours depend on pro-business climates in order to be successful, and we are honored to participate in the growth and success of China.

Q: What's your expectation for China and what's your ambition in the Chinese market?

M: We will continue expanding sales, production and sourcing, with a great emphasis on localizing our operations. As part of our long-term commitment in China, we will also continue looking for ways to contribute to society and give back to worthwhile causes. We will also strive to do our best to exceed the expectations of our Chinese customers, and continue to try and enhance our operations every day.

Q: What's China's significance to your company as well to yourselves?

W: China is a very significant market for us not only because of its rapid growth, but also because it is changing the way we interact with one another and how we see the world. In addition, we are also impressed by the Chinese people and their commitment to hard work, their emphasis on education, their optimism as they look toward a brighter future and the smiles they give whenever they say "hello".

We are very impressed with the central government's stated goal of promoting sustainable development. We share the goal of sustainable mobility in the technology of the vehicles we are developing, as well as how we do business.

By LI FANGFANG

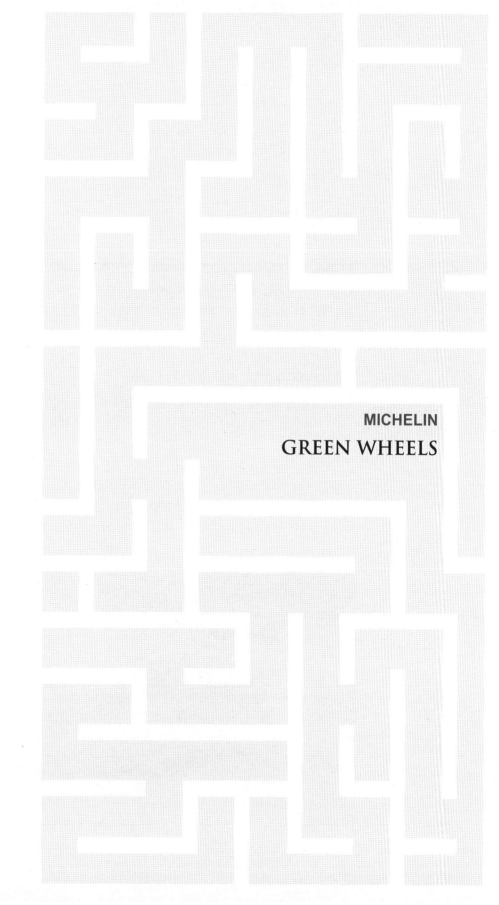

MICHELIN
GREEN WHEELS

It was far beyond Yves Chapot's expectation that after only two years, his company Michelin delivered the 100,000th "green" truck and bus tire to Chinese consumers.

Since it introduced its fuel-saving tires to China's commercial vehicle market (the world's biggest) in 2006, the French tire maker has made energy conservation and environmental protection a point of pride for its new products.

"China's 11th Five-Year Plan (2006-2010) calls for cutting energy consumption per unit of gross domestic product up to 20 percent by 2010. Michelin is making its own efforts under the Chinese government's guidelines," says Chapot.

Michelin Man Bibendum and a clean energy vehicle at Challenge Bibendum, one of the world's most important events Michelin hosted to promote the development of clean energy, road safety and fuel-efficient economy.

According to Michelin, with more than 400 million sold since its European launch in 1992, the green tires represent three-fourths of Michelin's sales in Europe. By replacing the carbon black in the tire treads with silica, the green tire guarantees a three percent saving on fuel consumption, thereby enabling the tire to maintain the same level of grip while reducing heat loss.

Michelin Man, the company's mascot and advertising logo, known as Bibendum, was created in 1898.

"Green tires take up two thirds of our replacement market in China. Most of the tires we offer here are of lower rolling resistance," Chapot adds.

Michelin is the only tire maker providing green wheels for trucks and buses in China. Industry forecasts say that by 2010 the total tire demand in the Chinese market will be around 300 million units. The demand will inevitably speed up and also hasten the application of environmentally friendly technologies.

"We think the road mobility in China is facing great challenges which result from a shortage of energy as well as traffic problems. We hope the green tire will contribute to improving the road situation in China," says Chapot.

To publicize its efforts in China, Michelin chose Shanghai to host its 2004 Challenge Bibendum, which was considered one of the world's most important events promoting the development of clean energy, road safety and fuel economy. Michelin's late CEO Edouard Michelin founded the event in 1998 to celebrate the 100th birthday of the Michelin Man, the company's mascot and advertising logo, known as "Bibendum".

GROWING
W I T H
CHINA
MNC EXECUTIVES
TALK ABOUT CHINA

182

The event returned to China again in 2007.

"The return to China was one way for Michelin and our partners to help the Chinese government chart the way forward for more fuel-efficient, cleaner, safer and less congested roads, an atmosphere that respects both people and the environment," says Chapot.

"In the future, we will continue to contribute to local communities with very strict respect to the environment and concrete commitments to local development and specific needs," he says.

Michelin has sunk US$440 million into the Chinese market since 1996. "The investment in China has proved to be the correct decision for Michelin," says Chapot.

Michelin was the first international tire maker to set up its office in China.

After establishing its sales office in Hong Kong in 1988, Michelin set up its first mainland representative office in Beijing in 1989 to promote its products and prepare the distribution channels in major cities.

"It showed Michelin's confidence in China and the local market. The reform and opening-up policy offered a good opportunity to Michelin by providing a favorable business investment environment," says Chapot.

However, in the early days, "how to level the cultural differences and combine Michelin's company culture with China's developing environment was the big challenge for Michelin", he says. "Michelin needed to build up a strong local management team."

In the late 1980s, a personal automobile was still out of reach for most Chinese people and as a result China's tire industry was in its infancy and professional talent was scarce.

"In the early 1990s, most of the Chinese managers' knowledge about management was quite limited, so Michelin Group sent over 10 managers from France," says Chapot. "It leveraged the strengths and weaknesses between different cultures and the knowledge spread better and faster inside the company."

The company later also sent Chinese employees to France for training. "We understood the challenge very well from the beginning. That was why most of the people that Michelin Group sent to China were not managers but technology experts," adds Chapot.

However, today, 15 Chinese are now working in high-level positions in France and other regional headquarters. In China, it has 5,500 employees and plans to hire more as its business expands.

In 1994, the Chinese government jump-started the country's auto industry development with a policy officially sanctioned, which for the first time put forward that the private purchase of vehicles be encouraged to change the sedan consuming restructure, linking cars with the family. Before that, sedans in China were limited to be sold to the public. They were majorly produced for official usage.

GROWING
W I T H
CHINA
MNC EXECUTIVES
TALK ABOUT CHINA

184

Passenger car production in 1995 increased 85,000 units over 1994, more than the total production volume of 1991.

At the end of 1995, Michelin's first joint venture operation in China, Michelin Shenyang Tire Co. Ltd., was established and it was transformed into a wholly foreign-owned enterprise in 2003. The total investment currently reaches US$150 million.

In 1998, China became the 10th largest auto market in the world. More auto manufacturers came to China, establishing production facilities to grab market share.

In April 2001, Michelin Group and Shanghai Tire and Rubber Co. Ltd. formed a new joint stock company, Shanghai Michelin Warrior Tire Co. Ltd., for the manufacture and sales of radial passenger car tires with a total investment of US$200 million.

The company produced domestic Warrior brand tires and started to produce Michelin brand tires in 2002.

Michelin's headquarters in China moved to Shanghai in 2001. In the same year, Michelin (China) Investment Co. Ltd. was set up in Shanghai, which gave the company more opportunities to develop and reinforce its long-term commitment in China.

"In 1990, the car inventory in China was 5.5 million. Now the number is up to 160 million. The fast developing the Chinese market gave Michelin a big sales volume increase," says Chapot, declining to disclose specific figures.

Michelin staff provides free tire check to the customers.

"But we have to use different ways to solve problems. In Europe, it usually takes us half a year to make a decision since the market is quite stable and the strategies are often made for the long term. But in China, we may make it in six weeks. The development and changes in China are very fast, so Michelin should make new decisions more actively and specifically," he adds.

GROWING
W I T H
CHINA
MNC EXECUTIVES
TALK ABOUT CHINA
186

Michelin's top rivals in China are US-based Goodyear and Japan's Bridgestone. The three brands occupy 60 percent of China's tire market. However, Chapot thinks there is still huge potential for Michelin to develop.

"For example, the truck tire market is the largest in the world, while the radial tire only takes 25 percent of the share. Moreover, the passenger and light truck market is held by international brands or local brands, while the truck tire market is dominated by domestic brands," he says, implying the segment will be Michelin's target in the future.

"Michelin's goal in the passenger and light truck market is to grow faster than the market average to keep our leading position."

Safety Priority

Q: What makes a tire company care so much about safety?

A: According to our statistics, tire problems cause 46 percent of accidents on expressways worldwide. And today China has the world's second largest highway network. Tire blowouts are the source of 70 percent of all accidents here.

Moreover, in 2004, after we set up the first automobile tire safety testing center, we found that 91 percent of the vehicles had tire problems.

Q: What made Michelin decide to make safety its core mission?

A: Safety has been one of our strategic objectives, and it

Yves Chapot,
Chairman of Michelin China

is very important for our global mission of maintaining sustainable mobility. Safety is beyond R&D and marketing. It actually relates to our sales channels and network. This is because we provide not only safe tires and safety services, but also safe driving concepts for drivers and tell them how to take care of their tires. So, safety is not merely about product and service. Most importantly, it is our responsibility.

Q: What is the biggest difficulty you have encountered in China?

A: My personal mission is to guarantee our Chinese staff and teams can continuously satisfy Chinese customers' requirements. We should know what kind of products and services our clients really need and their different requirements. Therefore, to understand our clients'

GROWING
W I T H
CHINA
MNC EXECUTIVES
TALK ABOUT CHINA

188

needs and meet their demands are the biggest challenges for us and also my personal mission.

Q: The recent price hikes in China include steel, gasoline, and logistics. How do they affect the cost of Michelin tires?

A: The tire industry has been affected by the rising cost of resources over the past few years. Yet the increase of the CPI in China has been more about consumer goods, and the increase in the cost of resources has been relatively lower than before. However, the increase in vehicle fuel prices will affect our consumers and that's why we are very focused on energy savings.

By LI FANGFANG

NOKIA
NOKIA RECHARGES

F ew foreign companies have gained the same success in China as Nokia has. The Finnish mobile phone vendor recently announced that it sold 70.7 million handsets in China in 2007, an increase of 38.6 percent year-on-year. Its market share reached over 35 percent in the country.

It not only knocked off multinational peers such as Motorola that used to dominate China's cellphone market, but also beat hundreds of domestic catch-ups that were theoretically better positioned to cater to local needs and domestic distributors.

Since 2005, China has been Nokia's largest single market and the country's huge low-cost manufacturing and design capacity has sustained the company's clout in the global market. However, Colin Giles, Nokia's senior vice-president and president of Nokia China, says it was still a surprise in 2005 when China became Nokia's biggest player.

"At that time, many thought the United States would be the biggest, so to some extent it was a surprise," Giles says. "But in all of our plans and forecasts, it is clear that China will continue to be the world's biggest market for mobile phones and play a very strong role in the industry globally."

Unlike Motorola, Nokia had a humble start in China. Although it opened its first office on the mainland in 1985, its international peers later overshadowed its debut with brick-like mobile phones that dominated the Chinese market from the late 1980s to the early 1990s.

The company's business saw a turnaround in 1994 when Wu Jichuan, the then Minister of Communications, Posts and Telegraphs, was invited to make a test call during an industry forum based on the GSM technology with former Nokia CEO Jorma Ollila, who sensed an opportunity in China's upcoming second-generation mobile network and decided to increase the company's investment in the country.

Nokia boosted its presence when it built additional factories and established joint ventures with local partners.

First Impressive Ad

In the early days of China's mobile phone market, handsets were only seen as a tool to make calls. People had little idea about cellphone brands because the phones were government allocated and not sold directly.

Giles says Nokia was not well known at the time. "And those consumers who knew about Nokia thought it was a Japanese brand," he says.

In order to establish connection between its brand and Chinese consumers, Nokia initiated its first successful TV advertising campaign in the country.

GROWING
W I T H
CHINA
MNC EXECUTIVES
TALK ABOUT CHINA
192

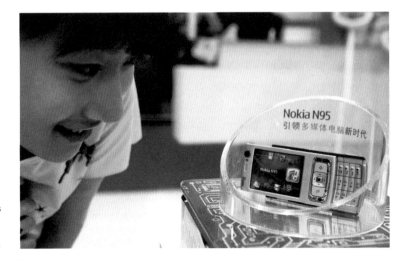

A visitor to a technology show looks at N95, a flagship multimedia mobile phone made by Nokia.

It featured two European-style statues in a park with a man sitting behind them on a park bench. A phone rang and people thought he was going to pull out his mobile phone, but he didn't. One statue pulled out a mobile phone and said, "Hello?" then turned to the other and said, "It's for you. It's your mama."

Although the ad seemed a little eccentric to most Chinese consumers who had been used to plain advertisement slogans, it was quite popular and many Chinese still remember it today.

"Actually, as for that particular ad, we were focusing on our European credibility. We are a European company, not Japanese," Giles says. "I think it also developed a very fun, humorous and human side of Nokia and it helped to develop the brand position during those years."

Boosted by the marketing campaign, Nokia's revenue surged in the following years as the country built up its second-generation network that significantly promoted the use of mobile phones.

According to figures from the National Bureau of Statistics, mobile phone users reached 13.23 million in China in 1997. The number grew to 43.3 million by 1999, with over 90 percent of them using handsets from global companies such as Motorola and Nokia.

Stumble Business

After a rapid growth in the late 1990s, Nokia's business was seriously challenged in China in the early 2000s.

By the end of 1998, the Chinese government mandated a licensing system for mobile phone manufacturers in an effort to encourage the development of domestic players.

The new manufacturers quickly swept the market with products that had acceptable quality at a much lower price. They also occupied the emerging rural market that the international mobile vendors hadn't yet tapped.

By 2003, market share of domestic mobile phone manufacturers surpassed 55 percent, according to figures from the government, and squeezed many foreign players such as Siemens, Alcatel, and Panasonic out of the market.

For Nokia, the challenge came mainly from product design and distribution strategy. During that time, Nokia hadn't paid enough attention to the emerging trend for clamshell phones, much different from the company's classic straight handsets.

GROWING
W I T H
CHINA
MNC EXECUTIVES
TALK ABOUT CHINA

194

The company also suffered from a centralized distribution system that no longer worked for the emerging rural market where potential users were highly scattered.

Lucky Trip

Nokia had planned an aggressive price reduction plan to combat the loss but the idea was scrapped after Giles happened to be visiting Chengdu in Sichuan Province.

During the four-day trip, he visited a mobile phone street (most Chinese cities have at least one mobile phone street packed with cellphone vendors) and talked to many there, including operators, distributors, shop clerks, sales people and merchandizing people.

He discovered that Nokia's rigid distribution strategy prevented consumers from getting its products.

"I had agreed with my boss, who was based in Singapore at the time, to make some changes in our pricing and make our pricing strategy a bit more aggressive," he recalls.

"When I was in Chengdu, I called him up and said, 'Cancel it. The problem is not that we need to be more aggressive in pricing. We need to ensure we have the right products to market through the right customer understanding, and we need to completely reconfigure our distribution systems to improve the way we manage retail.'"

After that, Nokia has started to revamp its distribution channel by reducing the number of national distributors while increasing the domestic or provincial distributors.

It also hired third-party sales representatives and opened its own-branded shops.

Meanwhile, the company aggressively increased its R&D activities in China, which significantly accelerated the company's response to the market needs.

In the following years, Nokia regained its momentum and its sales revenue surged from about 2.6 billion euros in 2004 to 6.4 billion euros in 2007, accounting for 13 percent of its global revenue.

"Our industry is built upon scale, so you need to have a certain percentage of the world's market share," Giles says.

New Era

Nokia is still reinventing itself in a new era when Internet and mobile phones are converging.

At the end of 2006, the company announced it was entering the world of the Internet with an Internet tablet, a wireless appliance that would allow the user to browse the Internet and communicate using Wi-Fi networks or mobile phones via Bluetooth. The move aimed to fight increasing challenges from new players such as Apple Inc, Google Inc and Amazon. China, which has the world's largest Internet population, is a market that Nokia cannot afford to lose on this new battleground.

"The most compelling change for us is the move toward the Internet," says Colin. "That story has already begun."

GROWING
W I T H
CHINA
MNC EXECUTIVES
TALK ABOUT CHINA

196

In the Beginning ...

Colin Giles is undoubtedly a legend in China's competitive mobile phone industry. He was the helmsman who engineered the turnaround of Nokia's mobile phone business in China.

While many foreign giants such as Alcatel, Siemens and Panasonic pulled out of the market, Nokia has maintained a firm leadership and its gap with the closest rivals has been widening thanks to Giles, who was senior vice-president of Greater China from January 2004 until the end of 2007, after serving as general manager of Nokia Mobile Phones, China, for two years.

In a recent interview, Colin Giles, who is now senior vice-president overseeing Nokia's eastern hemisphere business and still maintains the role of president of Nokia China, talked about Nokia's China odyssey.

Q: Were there some interesting stories when you first came to China?

A: One of the most interesting things I had was about visiting the post office.

This was already a new experience because where I come from you lick a stamp and put it on the envelope to send a letter out. So it was new to see people using paste to stick the stamp to the envelope.

Something even more interesting was that inside the post office there was one section allocated to stamps and letters and the other part was for SIM card.

This was well before China Telecom and China Mobile were separated and the whole Post and Telecom Bureau moved away.

At that time there were also a lot of entrepreneurial retailers that sought opportunities from this SIM card allocation, and they started setting up tables outside the post office to sell phones on the street to people who came out of the post office. That was in early 1995-1996, after mobile phone allocation ended. You could now choose phones.

Colin Giles,
Nokia's senior
vice-president and
president of Nokia
China

What is interesting is that I am always reminded of this experience because no matter which city I go to, there is always a mobile phone street.

This mobile phone street, which is very unique to China and does not exist anywhere else in the world, evolved from these tables that were set up outside the post offices.

Then the more entrepreneurial individuals set up shops next to the post offices, so they all developed around the post offices. These post offices then moved away, leaving a mobile phone street. And it all started from these tables!

Q: Nokia was struggling in China in 2002 and 2003. What were the main reasons?

A: I think there were many factors.

At some point we stumbled a little in understanding the Chinese consumers.

In 2002, about 40 domestic manufacturers entered the markets, who were clever companies that already understood China really well, had great track records in other categories of products, had strong brands, understood distribution, and were able to establish the right kinds of relationships at both international and local level.

So, the dynamic of our industry changed significantly during that period.

Q: What do you mean by stumbling in understanding the Chinese consumers?

A: There were a few elements at that point. One of them was product and the product designs like the clamshell phones. But it also related to an understanding of how distribution worked in China.

More than in any other market, retail plays a very strong role in China. So we had to understand distribution by retail, how that whole dynamic worked, and ensured that we would have the right kind of manpower to support those changes in distribution, and in 2003 we made several changes in our sales organization.

Q: What did you do to change your distribution system?

A: The fundamental change was to reduce our number of national distributors. Then we increased the number of domestic or provincial distributors.

We also changed their role from provincial distributors, and today we call them fulfilment distributors because primarily the distributors are logistics fulfilment houses that also offer credit and trade terms to the retailers.

We then have sales forces. We have about 1,500 sales representatives who are third-party employees, and they serve the retailers. We manage the retail together with the distributors, but their primary role is logistics fulfilment.

We also directly supply the organized retail chains, so working directly with them is also a major part of our business today.

We work closely with the operators and directly supply them in some cases.

Today we have about 130 dedicated Nokia shops. These are usually run by third parties, and if you walk into them you will find they are selling 100 percent Nokia phones.

Q: Nokia didn't enter China's rural market until 2005. Why didn't you do it earlier?

A: There were two reasons we didn't move into third- and fourth-tier cities before 2005.

One was that our business was already challenged in 2002 and 2003, so even at that point we had to stand back and reevaluate the business practices we had in the big cities.

GROWING
W I T H
CHINA
MNC EXECUTIVES
TALK ABOUT CHINA
200

From some perspective, we had no bandwidth to do it simultaneously in the rural areas. We decided to focus on the top 50 cities, so there was a conscious decision to focus on these cities in 2003-2004. Secondly, I would argue that the rural markets themselves weren't developing much either.

There was still very low penetration, and they were just starting to develop. So the timing might not be right anyway, but we weren't ready yet. There were definitely products being sold in those markets, but the volumes were still relatively small.

Q: **Where will Nokia in China go in the next 10 years?**

A: The most compelling change for us is the move towards the Internet. That story has already begun. We have seen strong convergence towards handsets with cameras, music players, GPS navigation capabilities, gaming, and email.

All of these new types of services are being integrated into mobile phones, so the mobile phone is no longer just a phone. In addition, as we move toward the Internet and the new services it allows, the device will become an even more central part of the way consumers conduct their lives.

These features together create a very rich mobile experience. I think the Internet itself will drive a lot of new types of services and technologies that you would be able to use on your mobile device.

By WANG XING

P&G
MASS APPEAL

GROWING
W I T H
CHINA
MNC EXECUTIVES
TALK ABOUT CHINA

202

It was in 1989 that people in major Chinese cities saw the first TV advertisement for Head & Shoulders shampoo and remembered the slogan, "Dandruff is gone, leaving more beautiful hair".

The shampoo, made by the United States-based Proctor & Gamble (P&G), was regarded as a luxury even for city dwellers in China at that time who even bought it as a gift on special occasions such as the Lunar New Year.

But two decades later Head & Shoulders is routine for many Chinese consumers, including rural residents who, in addition to Head & Shoulders, use Tide detergent, Safeguard soap, Crest toothpaste, Olay cream and Pampers disposable diapers.

"We started with one brand when we entered the market (in 1988). We now sell 22 brands. We started with a very small business (in China, but) this is now the second largest business for P&G in the world in terms of the volume of products we sell," says Christopher D. Hassall, vice-president of P&G China.

Hassall also notes that the world's leading consuming products manufacturer is growing along with the social and economic development of the nation.

According to Hassall, the fundamental thing for P&G in China is building brands. What P&G does is use its global knowledge and apply it in a localized manner to provide the brands that meet the needs of local consumers.

When P&G began its business in China, it focused on the area around its Chinese headquarters in Guangzhou, in south China's Guangdong Province.

It had a very disciplined expansion, first moving to other major cities, then moving into second- and third-tier cities and towns, and into the countryside.

The road has paralleled China's progress, from coastal areas, to cities in inner regions, and then to western and middle regions.

Pantene new line launched.

Accordingly, P&G's brands in China have extended from Head & Shoulders and Rejoice shampoos, to Olay and SKII skin care products, then Tide detergent and Crest toothpaste. And its growth has also been accompanied by intensified competition with arch rival Unilever and domestic players such as Nice and Liby in the emerging rural markets.

Gao Jianfeng, senior partner of Shanghai-based fast-consuming products market research firm Rona Consulting, says P&G is a company of brands. The Fortune 500 Company now operates over 300 brands in more than 160 nations and regions. And its differentiation and down-to-earth branding strategy contributes greatly to its success.

Advertising is a key tool for P&G to establish its brands globally and it is no exception in China.

In 1999 P&G China's advertising budget exceeded 500 million *yuan*, accounting for 10 percent of China's household and personal care chemical industry as a whole, sources from China National Light Industry Council say.

China Central Television (CCTV) started inviting bids for prime time ad slots in 1994, and P&G China was the top advertiser for four consecutive years during 2004-2007 by spending 380 million *yuan*, 385 million *yuan*, 349 million *yuan* and 420 million *yuan* respectively.

The ad blitz during prime time on TV, at prominent outdoor advertising sites, as well as on front pages of newspapers and magazines has worked well helping audiences remember a series of P&G brands.

"We have devoted conscientious effort to making our advertisements in such a way that they connect with the ordinary people more. Back in 1989 the advertisements were targeting the affluent consumers while now they are emotionally very in tune with the ordinary people," says Hassall.

In 1989's Head & Shoulders slot, the actress was a fashionable young lady, while the present Safeguard soap ad portrays an ordinary housewife dedicated to her baby and husband.

"We communicate in ways which are relevant to the consumers in China. We really do build the emotional connection between brands and consumers," Hassall adds. "P&G has been developing a series of brands to meet the needs of the very diverse population across China, from the very sophisticated consumers who live in cities to those consumers who live in the countryside and the rural areas who have more basic, fundamental needs."

For example, there are five hair care brands under P&G in China: Head & Shoulders focuses on fighting dandruff, Rejoice highlights soft and elegant hair, VS Sassoon promotes professional, designer hair care, Pantene concentrates on healthy hair and Clairol's promoting point is herbs and natural ingredients.

Hassall points out that his company is also a master at developing a single brand with different versions for different consumer groups in China, a nation with vast land, huge population base and diversified income levels and life styles.

GROWING
W I T H
CHINA
MNC EXECUTIVES
TALK ABOUT CHINA

206

Take Crest toothpaste: P&G has marketed Crest for over 10 years in China.

At the primary stage, particularly in rural areas, there was not a lot of awareness of the need for daily tooth brushing. One of the things P&G did was partner with the Ministry of Education and the Ministry of Health on building awareness about good oral hygiene.

Now for affluent urban consumers who are more affluent and live in cities, Crest is promoted more as a breath freshener that also helps keep teeth white and gums healthy.

It even uses traditional Chinese medicine ingredients in some versions of Crest, for example, the herbal versions and the "salt white" versions.

Another example is Tide detergent. For a rural consumer, removing tough stains is the primary need, so the product — High Clean White Tide — focuses purely on that and was developed at an affordable price.

For a consumer living in key cities with a washing machine and with less time to spend on the laundry, additional benefits like whiteness, softness and freshness are needed so P&G promotes other versions of Tide with additional functions and, of course, a higher price.

The most successful brand for P&G in China might be Olay skincare cream, which is also made in China and has also become one of the key products for the company in its global market. Olay is ranked as one of the

13 brands for P&G with annual sales exceeding US$1 billion, according to Rona's Gao.

A report by domestic research firm CCID Consulting says that sales in China's household and personal care chemical market amounted to 89 billion *yuan* in 2007, and forecasts that it will reach 218 billion *yuan* by 2015, with annual growth rate of 12 percent. Rona's research shows China's hair care sector chalked up 22 billion *yuan* in 2006, around 65 percent of which was made by P&G.

"When we decided on August 18, 1988, to enter China, it was a small investment, but we at that point saw tremendous opportunity. While it wasn't visible at the time, we truly think now that it is one of the wisest decisions that P&G has ever made," says Hassall.

Booming in China

China, without doubt, presents enormous opportunity for most multinationals. However it is a formidable challenge for many, especially for the consumer brands, due to the country's geographic diversity. P&G, since its entry into China in 1988, has long been a big winner. It's now one of the best-known brands in China, virtually in almost every corner from the metropolitan centers to the vast countryside.

In a recent interview with *China Business Weekly* reporter, Christopher D. Hassall, vice-president of P&G China, shared his insight on the Chinese market as well as the company's formula for success.

GROWING
W I T H
CHINA
MNC EXECUTIVES
TALK ABOUT CHINA

208

Q: What keeps a company like P&G increasing its investment in China?

A: One of the things I've found important is the partnership
with the government. I think that the regulatory environment and the legal framework have been much developed
here in China since 1978 when the country opened up.

The regulatory systems have been much more in sync
with global systems for developed market economies.
There are not only the regulatory and legal frameworks
but also the can-do attitude and partnership with the
government. I really do credit a lot to the local government and central government's professionalism in making China an attractive and predictable place to invest.

Q: In the past, P&G products were luxuries for many
Chinese. But now most can afford them. How has your
market strategy changed (especially for rural areas)?

A: When we started, we really focused on southern China
around our headquarters in Guangzhou. We've had a
very disciplined expansion, first moving to all the other
major cities, then moving into second and third-tier cities and towns, then moving into the countryside.

The way we've done that is not only through our
own development but by developing business
partnerships as well. We have a network of distributors around China, which means we now serve
hundreds of millions of consumers and these are
consumers all across China, every province, every
municipality, every town, city, county, village, has access to P&G products now.

And the way we've done that is to work in partnership with these distributors, with the retailers, with suppliers, with our manufacturing and distribution systems, because almost every product we sell in China is made in China. We now have 10 manufacturing plants around China, which means we can very efficiently get those products to consumers at a very good value that they can afford.

Christopher D. Hassall,
Vice-president
of P&G China

Q: **A number of small domestic producers have been washed out of the market due to fierce competition in the past two decades. How has P&G survived the competition and helped shape the competitive landscape of the industry?**

A: In 1978, China was a State-driven economy. But now it is a market-driven economy. That's been a very rapid evolution over those 30 years. As part of that, consumers really are the winners, because they have more access to more products, more choices, and it also drives competition in that the company who provides the highest value products at the best price.

There are four key factors that help P&G stand out in the competition.

The first one is innovation: making brands that are not only functionally but also emotionally relevant to consumers.

The second is scale. We are the largest daily consumer products company in the world and we can mobilize

resources internally and externally so that we can purchase our raw materials at competitive prices.

The third is organization. In China we have 6,500 employees.

The fourth is the quality of our people. We recruit and develop the best talents in the industry so that the company is run by the best in the industry.

By LIU JIE

GROWING
WITH
CHINA
MNC EXECUTIVES
TALK ABOUT CHINA

212

Mark Douglas,
President of Rohm
and Haas, Asia-Pacific

For many multinationals, China has been on the front-line of their corporate strategies.

Yet with rising labor and raw material costs and the *yuan*'s appreciation, some are transferring their manu-facturing to India, something that could weaken China's status as the world's manufacturing hub.

For the US chemical giant Rohm and Haas, headed by Raj L. Gupta, one of the few Indian-born CEOs heading Fortune 500 companies, a shift to India seems a natural move, underscored by his announcement in 2007 to invest US$100 million in the South Asian country.

However, for Rohm and Haas' Asia-Pacific president Mark Douglas, the answer is different. "It's not about 'China or India'. It's about 'China and India'," he says. The reason behind that, according to Douglas, is that Rohm and Haas has been doing better with domestic sales.

Unlike many multinationals, which have been building factories in China to serve both local markets and exports, exports from Rohm and Haas China are "a very minimal part" of its business. "We never envisioned China as a world factory. And in fact even in India 90 percent of our products serve only local customers," says Douglas.

Beijing Eastern Rohm
and Haas Co. Ltd.

That means Rohm and Haas' operations in China and India would hardly compete for orders or investment deals. And in fact, in China, Rohm and Haas had a head-start thanks to its 1979 entry into Hong Kong, one year after the Chinese mainland opened its gates to foreign investors.

By comparison, in India, its expansion has just begun. It opened its first sales offices in Delhi and Mumbai in 1995.

Rohm and Haas's initial small Hong Kong facility was used for its electronic materials business and served as a springboard to jump into the Chinese mainland market. In August 1987, Thomas Patrick Grehl was assigned to Rohm and Haas' Hong Kong operation as a financial manager and soon became the negotiator to form a joint venture on the mainland. The joint venture was launched in 1988 as the Eastern Rohm and Haas De-

GROWING
W I T H
CHINA
MNC EXECUTIVES
TALK ABOUT CHINA

214

velopment Center. And it was one of the very first Sino-foreign cooperative joint ventures after the *Law on Sino-foreign Cooperative Joint Ventures* took effect in April 1988.

During the late 1980s and early 1990s, some foreign companies withdrew from the Chinese mainland. That could have been a blow to China's economy, which was just shifting into high gear. By 1989 China had absorbed just about US$17 billion in accumulated actual foreign investment. However, Rohm and Haas chose to stay. "We have always had a long-term commitment to China," says Douglas.

That proved to be the right decision. In 2007 the actual foreign direct investment (FDI) in China hit US$82.66 billion, a record high. If Rohm and Haas had chosen to leave China and return later, its competitiveness could have been undermined.

In fact, the company has grabbed an upper hand by committing to China. It obtained the first license in Beijing to run a Sino-foreign cooperative joint venture, and because of that it benefited a lot from the preferential policies. At that time operating a cooperative joint venture, compared to an equity joint venture, offered the foreign investors much more flexibility in the way they managed their businesses and in their investment returns.

"It's paid off for Rohm and Haas to enter the Chinese market at the early stage when the country opened its door," says Douglas. "Time is money. The earlier we entered the market, the more time we have had to understand the market better, adjust our portfolio to match the local demand and gain local talents and finally establish our leading position in the country."

Rohm and Haas now bills itself as a special material company. And its electronic, painting, coating, packaging materials and performance materials are widely used in China. Rohm and Haas is hardly a household name, but without its technologies like plastic additives, many plastics would be brittle and vulnerable to flame and oxidation.

Rohm and Haas'
China Research and
Development Center.

In 2006, China contributed 40 percent to Rohm and Haas' sales in the Asia-Pacific region and it has formed 11 wholly-owned subsidiaries and joint ventures in China. In 2007, sales in China grew about 30 percent year-on-year, compared to an eight percent increase in global net sales.

With China becoming a major "growth engine", there is no reason for Rohm and Haas to shift its strategic focus from China to India even if it's coping with the rising prices of raw materials in China, says Douglas.

Underscoring the importance of China, five out of Rohm and Haas' seven vice-presidents for the Asia-Pacific region work in Shanghai, with the other two based in India and South Korea respectively.

Even when Rohm and Haas is making a slew of big deals in India, its investment in China has never seen signs of a slowdown.

In August 2007, Jinhong Rohm and Haas Chemical Company, a joint venture between Rohm and Haas and a local partner in Weihai, a city in Shandong Province, began operation to manufacture plastic additives. And in January 2008, a US$10 million plant in Sanshui, Guangdong Province, was launched to target the country's coating industry.

Douglas is now leading a mission to double the firm's sales in Asia-Pacific region to US$3.2 billion by 2010 compared to the 2006 figure, in which he says China will play the most crucial role.

And he is finding a new opportunity to goose Rohm and Haas' sales in China as the country is adopting a more environmentally friendly approach to develop its economy and trying to shed years of energy-guzzling model.

"On first thought, people always link pollution with chemical industries, which is not true. In fact you should know chemical companies help us improve our life quality with its advanced technologies," Douglas says.

A building and construction boom, sustained by China's economic boom, could also be a major revenue stream. That unit currently accounts for 30 percent of Rohm and Haas' total revenue globally.

By LI WEITAO

Schneider Electric

PLUGGED IN

GROWING
W I T H
CHINA
MNC EXECUTIVES
TALK ABOUT CHINA

218

In Jean-Pascal Tricoire's office in Paris sits a framed his-torical treasure, a well-marked French work certificate given to the late Chinese leader Deng Xiaoping.

"It's the most precious and historical stuff in my office as well as in my company. Moreover, it connects Sch-neider Electric with China, our most important market, from a long time ago," says Tricoire, chairman of the management board and CEO of the company.

With the certificate, France-based Schneider Electric's association to China can be traced back to the early 20th century, when the architect of China's reform and opening-up, Deng Xiaoping, while studying in France in his youth, worked for a time at the plant from which Schneider Electric grew.

In 1987, Schneider Electric established its first joint ven-ture factory, Tianjin Merlin Gerin Co. Ltd., in the north-ern costal city of Tianjin.

"Though China was at the very early phase of its reform period, Schneider Electric had confidence in the coun-try's prospects even then," says Tricoire.

The company has since established a strong foothold in

Schneider Electric celebrated its 20th anniversary of entering the Chinese market in Beijing, in August 2007.

the market over its two decades of development, growing together with the Chinese economy.

"Our company has invested roughly 15 billion *yuan* in China, which is by far the most important investment we've made in the history of Schneider Electric. There is no other country where in 20 years we would have invested that much money," says Tricoire.

Over the past decade the company has grown at an average annual rate of 20 to 30 percent, with a total tax contribution of five billion *yuan* to the Chinese government. "The speed with which the last 20 years has passed highlights the pace of our development," he adds.

"We have always brought the latest technology to China," says Tricoire. "Now with our R&D centers we are developing technologies from China that we are exporting and selling throughout the world."

The French company has established four branches, 38 regional offices, 21 production facilities, four distribution centers, one learning institute, two R&D centers, one Power Test laboratory, more than 500 distributors and a nationwide sales network in China.

"But this is an opportunity for us to look forward, and not just to reflect. We have a vision of our operations in China becoming a template for the future, both for Schneider Electric, and the power and control industry worldwide," he says.

A Witness to Changes

"Schneider Electric has witnessed the different phases in China's growth over the past 20 years, and has made it a part of its own mission to contribute to sustainable development of the economy," says Tricoire.

Actually in the early 1980s, before it established the first joint venture, Schneider Electric had already brought its circuit breaker technology to China, replacing the traditional fuse, and eventually setting new standards for circuit breakers in the country.

"It's the most outstanding contribution made by Schneider Electric to China. This move greatly enhanced the safety of power utilization and improved the living standard of the Chinese people," he says.

The company accelerated its expansion in China in the 1990s as the market opened further.

"In the period from 1992 to 2000, Schneider Electric set up in succession Schneider Electric (China) Investment Co. Ltd., the first R&D center, seven factories and three logistics centers. Our company's sales volume surpassed one billion *yuan* during this period," says Tricoire.

After years of discussions, Schneider Electric in December 2006 eventually formed a joint venture Delixi Electric Ltd. in Wenzhou, Zhejiang Province, with Delixi Group, China's second biggest low-voltage power distribution products supplier.

The venture, according to insiders, could be the biggest of its kind by scale and investment in China's power industry.

Schneider Electric also provided advanced product support and sophisticated technical services. The company's industrial products — such as low-voltage apparatuses, drives and contactors — were used extensively in the country's economic development.

"Since 2001, Schneider Electric embarked on all-around development in the Chinese market, keeping pace with the booming economy and supporting the country's development goals and priorities," says Tricoire.

The company has been involved in some of the country's largest engineering projects over the past two decades, including the Three Gorges Dam, the south-north water pipeline, the west-east gas pipeline and the Ling Ao Nuclear Power Plant.

It has also taken part in the construction of 47 main and

GROWING
W I T H
CHINA
MNC EXECUTIVES
TALK ABOUT CHINA

222

affiliated facilities of the Beijing 2008 Olympic Games, equipping them with energy-saving power solutions and automations to contribute the making of a 'Green' Olympics. The list includes the Bird's Nest, Water Cube, the new CCTV site, and the Beijing Capital Airport Terminal 3. In order to ensure smooth power delivery around the clock, Schneider Electric also stationed a full-day support team at various sports venues.

"Besides, we export from here, we buy from Chinese companies — from suppliers; actually, we buy more — in proportion — than we sell in China. China is the place where we source for components and we help Chinese companies export 60 percent of what we buy in China and what we buy is exported to other countries," says Tricoire.

"So we help Chinese companies elevate their quality levels, we help them export and we help them produce according to international standards."

Win by Local Cooperation

Tricoire uses the phrase "from partnership to prosperity" to conclude Schneider Electric's success in China. "We win in this unique market by cooperating with local companies."

"We have been working closely with local companies in manufacturing, as we sub-contract many things and it will also be that way for building solutions, because we must have agreements with local partners," he adds.

"We do that with local integrators, companies that work together with us, to adapt solutions to our customers' needs."

The country has been the No. 2 market in sales and numbers of employees in 2008 for Schneider Electric.

"People always look at the relationships between Chinese companies and international companies as competitions, but the story of Schneider here is that we always have very good cooperation with Chinese companies and those partnerships have lasted for very long and have been very fruitful."

Future Plans

Looking into the next 20 years, Tricoire smiles. "Personally, I think energy will be one of the biggest challenges for China from now to the future years. It's all about supervision, pollution and the capacity to support the development of China with the right amount of energy production and help China with its energy saving and emission control issues."

In August 2007, Schneider Electric celebrated the 20th anniversary of its first product series of Merlin Gerin's entry into the Chinese market.

The Chinese government included energy conservation in its 11th Five Year Plan (2006-2010), with a goal to reduce energy consumption by 20 percent per GDP unit by 2010.

"We believe that the best way to generate energy is to save energy. We are able to reduce electricity bills up to 30 percent with our technologies. On top of that, it contributes to reducing emissions," he says.

Schneider Electric has from years ago begun to shift its focus on supplying products to providing energy solution packages to China's customers.

The energy solution business now accounts for 10 percent of Schneider's Electric operations in China and is becoming more important for the company. "It may double in the coming year," Noel Girard, China marketing director of Schneider Electric tells *China Business Weekly*. Moreover, according to the CEO, Schneider Electric plans to increase its efforts in energy efficient solutions for the real estate sector.

"Certainly we provide the most complete system for energy efficiency in building today," says Tricoire.

Globally, Schneider Electric's real estate-related business contributes more than 50 percent to its overall turnover.

The company now sells its products to over 2,000 domestic real estate developers and has formed strategic alliances with more than 20 of China's major real estate firms, including Vanke and Wanda.

Past and Present

Jean-Pascal Tricoire has a deep emotional relationship with China, similar to his company's tight business connection with the country. He is one of the fairly few CEOs with the world's top 500 companies who can speak fluent Chinese, and even give a speech in Chinese. He spent five years in China from 1993 to 1998, when he was responsible for sales and when Schneider Electric expanded rapidly around the nation and established six joint ventures. He even has a common Chinese name, Zhao Guohua, which means China and shows his respect to China.

Jean-Pascal Tricoire,
Chairman and CEO of
Schneider Electric

Although he has taken over the global CEO position and has to shuttle around the 200 countries in which his company operates, Tricoire still visits China three or four times a year. During his recent visit to China, Tricoire talked to *China Business Weekly* reporter about his experience in China in the 1990s as well as his views on China's economic reform and opening-up.

Q: What's your view of China's huge changes in recent years?

A: I think China's change has been extraordinary in the past years. When I recall my first arrival in China in 1993, I can't recognize it. When I see what China has accomplished in past years: in terms of modernization, in terms of industrialization, in terms of the opening and integration into the world system, I'm amazed, puzzled and admiring. There have been huge changes in China, there will still be changes. I'm definitely very impressed at the way China is changing today.

GROWING
W I T H
CHINA
MNC EXECUTIVES
TALK ABOUT CHINA

226

I came for the first time here in China in 1993. When I was a kid, China was an inaccessible country. Before the "cultural revolution" (1966-1976), China was absolutely not accessible to the media. It was very difficult to understand what that meant in China. Then came the late 1970s and 1980s, when Deng Xiaoping, whom I greatly admire, called on China to open up. And then China started to open to the world, or the world started to open to China — a two-direction relationship. I was of the impression that at that time, it was difficult to under-stand what was coming from a different system. And then I came to China in 1993, (and what I saw) didn't correspond at all to what everyone was thinking.

Q: When you took over your company's sales in China in 1993, did you encounter any challenges?

A: I thought we had more opportunities than challenges in this country. In this country, our customers are very technical. But it is also a country where some of the national leaders are engineers. I envy that kind of country. In our country, politicians are normally profe-ssional politicians. What I mean by that is that (Chinese) people know what they speak in terms of technology.

What we see is that the Chinese market is very segmented. For very critical applications, very high-safety, high-reliability applications, Chinese engineers, Chinese design institutes and Chinese universities, we'd always chosen the best. So it took some time. We had to explain, we had people to test our products, then the confidence was established, the quality was proven, and we were able to value the price of our quality, the price of our technology and the price of our reliability. This is the most competitive market in the world. You've got people coming from America, you've got people coming from Japan, you've got people coming from Europe, so the best technology from the best competitors are here in China. So it's been on a day-by-day, customer-by-customer, people-by-people basis. I've mentioned, (that I had to) explain and establish the relationship of confidence, and (by this) I'm explaining the value of Schneider technology.

Q: What's your comment on your five years at Schneider Electric in China?

A: (After the first joint venture in Tianjin), from 1994 and 1999, we established six more joint ventures. That was a time of big industrial investment. Our biggest financial partnership was finding the right way of cooperation with our partners. This is the time also when we established a commercial cooperation: with distributors, with integrators — system integrators, with partner builders, with design institute — it was a time of very intense cooperation: upstream to produce our products with the highest quality; downstream commercially to get local companies use our products and customers to use our solutions.

Q: Then how about your career after you left China in 1999 and did your experience in China help you become Schneider Electric president?

A: First I went to work in South Africa to help in the development of Africa, then the US. After that I came back to Paris to be the general manager, then to be the president of the company. What's sure, I think, was what we did as a team, not me individually, but as a team in

GROWING
W I T H
CHINA
MNC EXECUTIVES
TALK ABOUT CHINA

228

China — not just my contribution but contributions of other members of the team in China, (which) includes a lot of Chinese people. Since then, I've been promoted and we've grown.

Q: As president of a global 500 company, what's your view on China's 30 years of reform and opening-up?

A: I think China is going in the right direction. Since I left in 1999, China entered into the WTO, which was a big change, to make China international. China has kept on opening in terms of economy and infrastructure. I believe that the Olympic Games taking place in Beijing was a very good thing because it rewarded China's strong and fast opening and integration to the world. I think it's a very good symbol of all the changes that happened in the past 25 or 30 years in China.

The quality of infrastructure here is becoming excellent. It's top of the world standards — the airports, the stations and the highways. These are becoming top-class, world class. We are meeting people who know this is the biggest country for foreign investments for many years. People are very used to foreign investments from many countries so it's becoming easier and easier to establish an operation here and I can say this is going in a very good direction. This is a very competitive place to do business.

By LI FANGFANG

MEETING IN THE MIDDLE

Shell's external affairs director Liu Xiaowei still clearly recalls what happened in 1997 when Shell set up a joint venture fuel storage business.

She asked that the workers wear protection equipment such as safety shoes and hard hats only to find that no one complied.

Until she told them that they could be fined for not wearing safety gear, one worker told her that his safety shoes were so posh that he wanted to save them to wear for his wedding ceremony.

"It took a long time to bring the concept of safety protection to China," she says.

Indeed, it took a while for Shell to blend its concepts and culture with its local partners, and it also took a long time for Shell to localize its business.

When Shell reopened an office in Beijing (it had been in China before 1949 when the People's Republic of China established) in the 1980s, it was a small place with six or seven employees, only involved in trading.

Liu remembers when she joined Shell in the 1990s,

Shell China's headquarters was based in Hong Kong, and its CEO was a British citizen who could not speak Chinese. There was not a single Chinese manager, either.

"It was hard work in China because the country was in its initial period of opening-up at that time," Shell China's executive chairman Lim Haw Kuang says of the first time he visited the mainland in 1996.

"Anything to do with energy was regulated. So you couldn't run your business the same way as you did in the West."

But one year later, Shell moved its headquarters to Beijing and in 2000, and appointed a Malaysian Chinese to lead its operation in China.

"You can see Shell's changing attitude towards China by nominating CEOs from a relatively closer area," says Liu.

Shell is a top international energy company with the widest range from upstream to downstream.

It has jointly developed the Changbei gas field with PetroChina in northwest China and delivered natural gas to Beijing, Tianjin as well as Shandong and Hebei provinces.

It also became a leading international oil company in China's lubricant market in 2006, following the acquisition of a 75 percent share of Beijing Tongyi Petroleum Chemical Company Ltd. and Tongyi Petroleum Chemical Company Ltd.

Lim Haw Kuang,
Executive Chairman of
Shell China

Turning Shell Around

Shell China's executive chairman Lim Haw Kuang is un-questionably an effective reformer for Shell China. He localized Shell China's leadership team with Chinese employees increasing from zero to a majority in three years, and engineered the turnaround of Shell's business in China.

"Ninety-eight percent of my colleagues are Chinese, 99 percent of my customers are Chinese, and 100 percent of government officials are Chinese, how long do you expect me to wait for the localization?" says Lim who has visited virtually all of China, save Guizhou Province.

"Our lubricant business, which consists of 100 percent of Chinese employees in China, is the second largest of Shell's globally."

But when Lim headed for China in 2005 to assume the helm for Shell China the company was bogged down in several large projects including a natural-gas pipeline it was working on with PetroChina and CNOOC.

In a recent interview, Lim Haw Kuang talked about Shell's growth and success in China.

Q: Would you like to relate your personal experience to reflect the changes in China?

A: My first experience in China in 1996 was as a visiting overseas Chinese here on business for Shell. When the plane touched down, I couldn't wait to touch the soil. The first stop was Beijing. There were lots of bicycles.

Now you can see places with Eastern and Western elements mixed, and you can find service that is absolutely first-class.

The way people dressed was pretty ordinary at that time. But now when you go to a shopping mall in Shanghai or Beijing or other major cities, you can imagine yourself as in anyplace like New York or London.

The business mindset has already changed. The mindset about receiving subsidies from the government has also changed.

But there is one thing that has not changed.

I have visited more than 30 provinces in China, even these poor and remote areas. There is one thing they all have in common — the focus on education. It is fantastic.

Q: How did Shell influence and was influenced by its joint venture partners? Could you provide an example?

A: Our HSE (Health, Safety and Environment) standards and practices in the Changbei Gas Project with PetroChina in Yulin, Shaanxi Province have been showcased by our partner in their internal communications as an example of the best HSE practices.

We also learn from Chinese companies that have unique operational expertise and work jointly to deliver more synergies.

For example, when we acquired Tongyi lubricants, we knew that it had a more efficient commercial model and

GROWING
W I T H
CHINA
MNC EXECUTIVES
TALK ABOUT CHINA
234

operational process. We kept the management team, the business model and process from Tongyi after the acquisition.

Q: What's your view on the challenge for Shell in China now?

A: When you come to a country or a market, you need to understand their priorities and values.

When I became the executive chairman of Shell China, I gave the same reply. (The) US$4 billion (we have invested in China) is a drop in the ocean. We are one of the world's top energy companies and we should work hard but we are not doing enough.

The challenge is also about the future leaders of the future organization. You need become quite focused on people's efforts.

In 2008, I will spend 50 percent of my time in managing people.

For me, the success of future is not about money, it is about people. I hope when one person mentions Shell, he/she will say that's a good company with good people.

Q: China is in pursuit of a more rational and efficient mode of growth. How can Shell China better get involved in such a drive?

A: Over the last 30 years China has experienced dramatic economic growth. Some people are asking when China will become the largest economic country in the world? Do you notice the question is not "if" but "when"?

By 2050, the world population will rise by 50 percent, but the energy demand will double.

If you look into the future, traditional energy such as coal and oil will still be the dominating energy-consuming source. Therefore, traditional energy will not be enough to meet the additional huge demand.

It is a global thing. But China might have more serious burden because China has the largest population in the world, and primarily bases its energy consumption on coal.

We want to be the leading international oil company contributing to the economic prosperity of China and our customers in a sustainable manner.

If you look at Shell's energy priorities, energy supply security, environmental protection and energy efficiency are three things we have done constantly.

Q: As we know, you engineered the turnaround of Shell's business in China, could you share the secret of success with us?

A: Three years ago when I started to head Shell China, there were no Chinese in the country's coordinating team (core management team). But now there are 10 Chinese staffers out of the 16 members of the team. This is very aggressive process. But when you want to localize your talents, you also have to internationalize them. I need Chinese talents who can also learn all the international expertise and who can compete internationally.

Q: What in your view will your biggest achievement have been when you leave China?

A: If everyone in Shell is very proud of Shell and himself or herself by the time I leave, I will be the happiest man in the world.

By ZHANG QI

Siemens

POWERING CHINA

GROWING
WITH
CHINA
MNC EXECUTIVES
TALK ABOUT CHINA
238

In Beijing's northeastern Wangjing District, close to the fourth ring road, a 30-story transparent building has become the new landmark of the district. It is the new headquarters of Siemens China, a one billion *yuan* site, which has come to represent the group's ambitions in the country.

"Our new home is a symbol of Siemens' long and lasting commitment to China. It reaffirms the strategic importance of China for Siemens' global business and the strong confidence that Siemens has in the Chinese mar-

Headquarters of
Siemens China

ket," says Richard Hausmann, president and CEO of Siemens China.

The German company has relations with China that go back to over 100 years ago and is now integrated into the market.

Its products, refrigerators and washing machines can be found

Siemens office building in Shanghai (1937). China was once the second overseas market Siemens entered after the company was set up in 1852.

in millions of Chinese households across the nation, but the group has also been committed to industrial initiatives in China.

It has provided environmentally friendly equipment for power generation and transmission in the country and also supplied China's railway system with locomotives for upgrades.

Today Siemens has more than 90 operating companies and 60 regional offices across China.

In fiscal year 2007, it added 7,000 staff members to its local operations, making it one of the largest foreign-invested enterprises in the country, with over 40,000 employees.

Now all the company's business segments worldwide have a presence in China, including automation and control, power, transportation, medical equipment, information and communications, lighting and household appliances.

GROWING
WITH
CHINA
MNC EXECUTIVES
TALK ABOUT CHINA
240

Delivery of the first
pointer telegraphs
in 1872 marked the
beginning of Siemens'
cooperation with
China.

In fiscal year 2007, the company's sales and new orders in China increased by 21 percent to 53.3 billion *yuan* and 60.7 billion *yuan* respectively. "We are on the way to reaching our ambitious goal of 100 billion *yuan* in annual orders by 2010," Hausmann says.

The company has also played an active role in both the Beijing Olympics in 2008 and the World Expo which will be held in 2010 in Shanghai.

It has secured 1.1 billion euros in orders for projects relating to the Olympic Games, such as a baggage handling system for the newly constructed Terminal 3 of the Beijing Capital International Airport, which will be used for the Olympic Games.

The company has signed an agreement to officially become the global partner for innovative infrastructure and healthcare for the 2010 Shanghai World Expo. It will provide technology, solutions and high-quality products and services to the expo, particularly in the areas of rail transportation, building technology and healthcare.

Siemens' long history of co-operation with China dates back to 1872. Twenty-five years after the company was founded, it delivered China's first pointer telegraph, marking the beginning of modern telecommunication development in China.

In 1974, Siemens received the first order from China since the late 1930s, providing 14 steam turbines to the country. In the same year, Siemens supplied the first set of advanced electrical control systems for the cold rolling mill of Wuhan Iron and Steel Company.

After China adopted the reform and opening-up policy, Siemens also increased its investment in the Chinese market. In 1985 the company signed the memorandum of comprehensive cooperation with the Ministry of Machinery, Electric and Electronics Industries of China. Siemens was the first foreign enterprise China invited to participate in such a comprehensive co-operation scheme.

Sinumerik 802S is developed and built in China for the Chinese and the global market by Siemens Numerical Control Ltd., Nanjing.

Richard Hausmann,
CEO of Siemens
North East Asia and
President and CEO of
Siemens Ltd. China.

In 1989 Siemens founded its first joint venture in China, Siemens Technology Development Corporation Ltd. This company provided after-sales, diagnostic and repair services for the growing installed base of Siemens' medical equipment in China.

In 1994 the company founded Siemens Ltd. China in Beijing, consolidating Siemens' rapidly growing operations and investment in China. It was the first holding company formed by a foreign group in China.

Now China has become the company's third largest market worldwide, after Germany and the United States.

"China is not only an important manufacturing center for us. We are also expanding our research and development in the country," says Hausmann.

The company has already started research and development (R&D) activities in China in all its fields of business. In 2004, Siemens established a corporate technology R&D center in Beijing, with the mission of developing unique innovations for Siemens business in China and worldwide.

In 2005, Siemens Medical Solutions Group announced it was to invest 300 million *yuan* to establish its Asia center of excellence in Shanghai, which would focus on the R&D, manufacturing, service and marketing for Siemens medical products such as CT, X-ray, ultra-sound and medical components. The center would become the focal point of all Siemens medical activities in China. And its development had implications for the company internationally.

"Covering both basic research and product development, our R&D work here not only benefits our Chinese market, but also the market worldwide," says Hausmann.

Green Development

Siemens has announced that it plans to inject half of its 10 billion *yuan* mid-term Chinese investment into energy-saving and environmentally friendly technologies and solutions in a move to expand its position in this field. "For Siemens China, we estimate that over 50 percent of our future growth will be related to green technology," Hausmann claims.

The company in the beginning of 2008 announced to reorganize its businesses into three sectors — industry, energy and healthcare.

The industry arm will comprise the business of industry automation, drive technologies, building technologies, industrial solutions, mobility and Osram, the lighting company. The healthcare sector will comprise the medical solutions group including imaging and IT, workflow and solutions, and diagnostics.

As for the energy business, it covers fossil power generation, renewable energy, oil and gas, energy service, power transmission and power distribution.

"Now our portfolio covers the entire energy chain with our energy-efficient products and solutions. Globally we have also invested in a wide range of alternative energy sources, from wind technology to fuel cells," says Hausmann.

At present there are approximately 6,300 Siemens wind turbines, which cut carbon dioxide emissions by 10 million tons a year, in operation worldwide.

"Siemens wind power is the world leader in offshore wind energy. We are in discussions with some Chinese companies for cooperation in the area of alternative energy," says Hausmann.

By WAN ZHIHONG

South Korea Chamber of Commerce

GROWING TOGETHER

GROWING
W I T H
CHINA
MNC EXECUTIVES
TALK ABOUT CHINA

246

When Woo Nam-kyun visited Beijing for the first time in 1983 it was his third year working for South Korea-based LG Electronics and he stayed in the Jian'guo Hotel.

He still remembers there was a tract of farmland across the street. Now there stands the 140-meter-high twin towers of LG (China), where Woo works as the president and CEO. The buildings resemble LG's headquarters in its home country.

LG took the initiative in investing in China in Huizhou, Guangdong Province, in 1993, with an initial investment of US$3.5 million.

"China's development in the past three decades is dazzling," says Woo, who is also Chairman of South Korea Chamber of Commerce in China.

Woo Nam-kyun, President and CEO of LG (China) and Chairman of South Korea Chamber of Commerce in China.

He says South Korean people are very proud of the fast growth achieved by their country, but China has recorded an even faster development since its reform and opening-up in 1978.

"It is very hard for a country with a large territory, much larger than South Korea, to maintain such fast growth," he says.

What has amazed the South Korean businessman is the fast urbanization in the country, which he describes as one of China's most significant achievements in its reform and opening progress. The living condition of Chinese people has been greatly improved, too.

Although South Korea established formal diplomatic relations with China in 1992, quite late in comparison with other Asian countries such as Japan and India, South Korean businesses wasted no time in cashing in on the opportunities.

As a major multinational in South Korea, LG took the initiative in investing in China in Huizhou, Guangdong

GROWING
W I T H
CHINA
MNC EXECUTIVES
TALK ABOUT CHINA

248

Province, in 1993, with an initial investment of US$3.5 million. Now the factory producing digital products, such as AudioHiFi, CDRom and DVDRom, provides about 10,000 jobs for the locals.

LG's investment in China, the first from South Korea, has stimulated investments by other South Korean businesses.

According to the statistics from South Korea, there are at least 40,000 South Korean companies investing in China with an accumulated investment of about US$100 billion. Established in 1993, South Korea Chamber of Commerce now has 6,000 members.

Woo says South Korean businesspeople regard China as an amiable and safe investment destination as the two countries are close in culture and South Korea also uses Chinese characters, known as hanja; (although not widely, as its own alphabet, Hangul, was created in the 1400s.)

"The polices the Chinese government offers to foreign investment are attractive," Woo says adding that China, as one of the world's largest economies, is also a big market.

During the past 16 years, China has become the largest trade partner of South Korea, which is one of China's top 10 trade partners.

Statistics from the Ministry of Commerce show China's exports to South Korea hit US$56.14 billion in 2007, up

26.1 percent from a year earlier while the country's imports from South Korea stood at US$103.75 billion, up 15.6 percent.

The relationship between the two countries has also been highly promoted. China and South Korea recently agreed to upgrade their "comprehensive and cooperative partnership" to "strategic cooperative partnership" during the latest summit talks between Chinese President Hu Jintao and his South Korean counterpart Lee Myung-bak.

"I think a strategic cooperative partnership means any decision by one side will impose a remarkable impact on the other," Woo explains.

At the earlier stage of their investment in China, South Korean businessmen, like many other foreign investors, focused on the manufacturing industry in a bid to take advantage of the labor and resources in the country. But Woo says they should adapt themselves to the changing circumstances.

However, differentiating themselves from other players does not mean they have to give up the manufacturing industry, Woo says. South Korean businessmen should take the business in China as a "cause" rather than simply a manufacturing facility.

For example, he explains, LG set up a joint venture in Shenyang, Liaoning Province in 1994, producing CRT televisions for both domestic and overseas markets.

GROWING
W I T H
CHINA
MNC EXECUTIVES
TALK ABOUT CHINA

250

While a number of Chinese people are replacing their CRT televisions with flat-screen TVs, the South Korean company hasn't shut the factory down. Instead, it has turned to developing markets abroad, such as Central and South America, India, East Europe and East Africa. "Now it does exports only and keep a very good profit margin," Woo says.

He says the company had spent a lot in training employees in the Shenyang factory, which helps its shift to new overseas markets.

As the newly elected Chairman of the South Korea Chamber of Commerce, Woo suggests that both governments speed up reaching a free trade agreement (FTA).

"The two countries should ink a free trade pact as soon as possible because such a pact will help sharpen the competitive edge of both countries by opening the markets to each other and sharing the resources," he explains.

The fifth round of joint study on a possible FTA was held in Beijing between June 11 and 13 with officials discussing a feasibility study that began in November 2006.

"In a long run, if we can form a free trade system among China, Japan and South Korea. It could be as influential as the North American Free Trade Area and the European Union," Woo says.

By JIANG WEI

TOSHIBA

GROWING WITH CHINA

GROWING
W I T H
CHINA
MNC EXECUTIVES
TALK ABOUT CHINA

252

Takaaki Tanaka's first visit to China is just a distant memory at best.

At that time, in 1990, the then corporate personnel manager of Toshiba traveled to Dalian as an advance man to establish a manufacturing base in the coastal city in northeastern China. All he can recall is a cluster of old streets, buildings, and bicycles as well as people strolling on the streets.

That is because he was immersing himself in Toshiba's strategic plans, both globally and in China.

"In 1990s we started regarding China as our major manufacturing hub to cut our costs at home in order to improve global competitiveness," says Tanaka, who is now chairman and president of the Japanese behemoth's China operations.

And Toshiba was lured by Dalian's geographic locale: it's the nearest Chinese costal city to Japan. Toshiba located the manufacturing facility in Dalian's Economic and Technological Development Zone, which boosted the firm's competitiveness with its preferential economic policies, including tax breaks.

A worker helps set up a Toshiba booth at a trade show.

GROWING
W I T H
CHINA
MNC EXECUTIVES
TALK ABOUT CHINA

254

Since then the facility has been churning out motors, radio tubes, television sets and medical equipments to supply Toshiba's sprawling operations across the world.

That was boon for Toshiba and China. The country was eager to attract foreign investment to boost its economy by establishing economic special zones and economic and technological development zones.

In fact, Dalian Economic and Technological Development Zone, which started construction in 1984, was the first of its kind in the country. The surging foreign investment, especially by Japanese companies such as Toshiba, has built the zone from a fishing village into a cluster of modern high buildings, and significantly transformed the skylines of Dalian and helped build it into one of the most dynamic cities in the country. It is a city which Tanaka can hardly recognize now compared to 18 years ago.

During 1995 and 1998 Tanaka oversaw Toshiba's Asian operations and witnessed another major shift in Toshiba's China strategy.

In 1995, Toshiba (China) Co. Ltd. was officially established, which shored up the Japanese company's management strength in China and facilitated the decision-making process. And its manufacturing facilities in China also started supplying the Chinese markets.

"China has grown into a major economic powerhouse in the world. We now are regarding China as a huge market, (not merely a manufacturing floor)," says Tanaka.

Underlining the dramatic change is the number of Toshiba's subsidiaries and joint ventures in the country that have grown into 69 from two in 1991 when Tanaka paid his second visit. And it has invested more than eight billion *yuan* and employed more than 25,000 people in China. Sales, including exports, hit 66.4 billion *yuan* in 2006.

Toshiba is putting China at the forefront in its overseas expansion plans. Underscoring that, Tanaka was assigned to lead the China operations in 2007 after serving as head of the Overseas Business Promotion Division of Toshiba for two years.

Power Play

Toshiba is putting a big bet on Tanaka, hoping his rich overseas experience can continue to boost its China sales.

Overseas markets, with the US and China being the top two, now account for about half of Toshiba's total sales.

Tanaka has mapped out an ambitious plan. He hopes China can overtake Japan as the largest country market for Toshiba within 10 years, fueled by China's strong purchasing power.

The firm is now on the track to achieve the goal. Its sales in China have been growing fast, and in 2007 they exceeded 80 billion *yuan*, beating a target of 79 billion set in 2006.

GROWING
W I T H
CHINA
MNC EXECUTIVES
TALK ABOUT CHINA

256

Tanaka says a major drive could be the sales of Toshiba's so-called "social infrastructure systems", mostly comprised power generation, transmission and distribution, industrial and environmental systems.

Currently sales of social infrastructure systems contribute 20 percent of Toshiba's total revenues in China, with digital products including home appliances accounting for 30 percent. The remaining 50 percent is from semiconductor-related sales.

"We are aiming to more than double the sales of social infrastructure systems by 2010 from 2006," Tanaka says.

That ambitious goal is based on China's increasing awareness of environmental protection and energy conservation, he explains.

In 2007, about 33 percent of Toshiba's worldwide sales were from "green" products. Toshiba predicts that they will be increased to 60 percent by 2010 and 80 percent by 2012.

"Demand for energy-saving and environmentally friendly products is surging both in Western countries and China. And we are ready to capitalize on the boom with our expertise," Tanaka says, adding he is excited by China's growing interest in nuclear power as an energy option.

China is now hoping that nuclear power could account for five percent of its power generation by 2020, which means it plans to build more than 30 new nuclear power reactors in the coming years — up from 11 now. And by

2050 the percentage could reach 50 percent in a bid to cut the proportion of water and coal-fired power plants.

In February 2006, Toshiba acquired Westinghouse Electric for US$5.4 billion, a move widely seen as part of its effort to tap into China's nuclear power boom, which could result in spending US$50 billion before 2020.

Before that, the Japanese company's expertise was in boiling-water reactors, which have been largely limited to the Japanese market.

Westinghouse holds orders to provide equipment to four nuclear power plants in Shandong and Zhejiang provinces, which bodes well for Toshiba. Toshiba has been a leading player in power transmission and distribution and the acquisition of Westinghouse could broaden its portfolio, which is improving the Japanese firm's overall competitiveness in China.

Despite the optimism, Toshiba is still facing a formidable challenge in cracking China's consumer electronics market, where it has been losing its luster.

In fact, Chinese have known the Toshiba brand since 1972, before the reform and opening-up policies of 1978 opened the floodgates to foreign brands.

After 1972 when China and Japan normalized their diplomatic ties, Toshiba started technology transfers and exports of medical equipment, broadcasting equipment and power equipment to the country.

GROWING
W I T H
CHINA
MNC EXECUTIVES
TALK ABOUT CHINA

258

In the 1980s it already grew into a household name with healthy sales of home appliances.

But since the late 1990s, it has been losing the battle-field to hard-charging local manufacturers, which have been aggressive in pricing, as well as South Korean companies, which have been quick to cater to local tastes in product designs. Tanaka is now trying to revamp the Toshiba brand to boost sales.

In 2007 Toshiba signed up Chinese diving queen Guo Jingjing as an image ambassador to promote its brand. That's a first for the Japanese company, although it's already an old trick by Chinese and South Korean firms.

Also the firm has launched 40 exhibition halls in major cities to promote its consumer products, which Tanaka says has started paying off.

However, the president acknowledges digital products, including home appliances, might contribute a smaller percentage to Toshiba's total sales in China given the price wars dogging the industry. That could reinforce the growing importance of social infrastructure systems, which promise much higher·margins.

Firstcomer

In 1978 China embraced the reform and opening-up policy, which gave multinationals the access to the world's most populous country and now the most dynamic market. However, Japan's Toshiba has a much longer presence than its peers as it already made its first foray in 1972 when China and Japan normalized their diplomatic relations. During an exclusive interview with *China Business Weekly* reporter, Takaaki Tanaka, chairman and president of Toshiba's China operations reviewed the firm's development in the country.

Takaaki Tanaka, Chairman and president of Toshiba China

Q: In 1995 you started overseeing Toshiba's Asian operations and in 2005 you took charge of Toshiba's overseas businesses. Now as chief of Toshiba's China operations, what changes do you think have happened to China's position in Toshiba's radar screen?

A: The trade between China and Japan has been on the rise since the two countries normalized their diplomatic ties in 1972. After China embraced the reform and opening-up policies, Toshiba exported industrial equipment, coal-fired power equipment and home appliances in large volume to China.

In the first half of the 1990s, Japanese companies including Toshiba, in a bid to cope with intensifying global competition and increase cost effectiveness, started direct investments in China and established a number of manufacturing bases.

In the second half of the 1990s, Toshiba started aggressively attacking China's domestic market and forging joint ventures with local partners. Since then we regarded China as the major market for our manufacturing facilities in the country.

In 2000 we started ramping up our marketing campaigns in China. Now we already have 69 subsidiaries or joint ventures compared to two in 1991.

GROWING
W I T H
CHINA
MNC EXECUTIVES
TALK ABOUT CHINA

260

Q: When looking back, what right decisions do you think
Toshiba has made in the past few years since 1972?
Was there any decision you feel regretful about?

A: I'm pleased Toshiba made its advance into China much
earlier than other Japanese companies. As a result,
Chinese people had chances to understand Toshiba's
brand and technologies as early as the 1970s and that
has established Toshiba as a premium brand in China.
For instance, we had been the No. 1 player in China's
office copier market for eight consecutive years. And
our catchphrase for TV commercials, broadcast starting
from the 1980s, remains fresh in many Chinese people's
memories.

However, an economic recession hit Japan in 1990s,
which put a brake on Japanese companies' overseas
sales and investments for about 10 years. In contrast,
investments by European and US companies shifted
into high gears and established their leading positions
in the infrastructure sector. In home appliance sectors
like television products, South Korean firms also made
great strides with their aggressive investment strategies.

Now Toshiba is in a fast lane with approximately 20
percent annual growth. We are facing stiff competition
but in a long term I'm quite optimistic about Toshiba's
prospects.

In a country with a history of more than 5,000 years,
it doesn't make sense if you make plans with predictions for just two to three years. When working on your
corporate plans, you should cast your sights on 2020 or
even 2050 and then come back to your three-year plans.

Recently I attended a forum in Beijing at which Zhang Guobao, Vice-Minister of the National Development and Reform Commission (NDRC), said China hoped its nuclear power generation could account for five percent of the total by 2020. In the power sector, even one percentage is a big thing. The goal means China would increase the number of nuclear power reactors to more than 30 from 11 now.

It is also said China expected nuclear power generation could account for half, with hydropower and coal-fired power sharing the remaining. The build-out of infrastructure needs a long-term plan. In terms of energy strategy, in particular, you need look beyond 2050 at least.

In fact, we make plans within each three years. That requires us to make the right predictions about what will happen to China by 2020 or even 2050.

Q: Multinationals are now coping with a growing number of challenges in China such as the unified income tax rate (for domestic and foreign companies) as well as the possible cost rise resulting from a new labor contract law. What's your comment on that?

A: The unification of the income tax rate and the introduction of the new *Labor Contract Law* are in line with the social development in China and indicate businesses are getting mature in the country.

Business activities have to be well planned. And businesses need some time to prepare for the new laws or regulations. We hope we could get enough time to

GROWING
W I T H
CHINA
MNC EXECUTIVES
TALK ABOUT CHINA

262

adjust ourselves before a new law or regulation is enacted and implemented. I suppose, that is a difference between Japan and China.

Anyway, as we have been upholding our corporate social responsibility guidelines, we will try our best to learn and understand China's laws and regulations and strictly observe them in our business activities since we are doing business in the country.

By LI WEITAO

Volkswagen
IN EARLY, ON TOP

Today China has the largest potential auto market in the world — with nearly all international brands setting up production and operations — but Volkswagen's position is unique.

It was the first foreign auto company to enter China and is still one of the biggest brands, with a leading position in the market. It is not only an eyewitness, but also an actor and contributor to the growing auto industry.

And since 2007, China has been Volkswagen's biggest market outside Germany.

Volkswagen's new Beetle car, one of the most favorable vehicles among Chinese female drivers.

"We want to keep the leading position in the years to come," says Winfried Vahland, president and CEO of Volkswagen Group China. "Our sales volume target for 2008 is one million. For the long term, we will bring more new technologies, products, and services to Chinese consumers."

Most Reliable Partner

"It has been 30 years since Volkswagen started to get in touch with the Chinese government. Looking back, Volkswagen and China opted to start their respective new eras with the right strategic decision with each other," says Vahland.

Volkswagen has been with China's auto industry since 1978 — the year the country began its economic reform and opening process.

It's also the year the Chinese government decided to rev up China's auto industry — it approved a proposal suggesting that China should enhance its auto production level by introducing the latest foreign technologies. The pilot site was in the Shanghai Sedan Plant — one of the few sedan producers at that time — with a goal to turn it into a modern auto production base and then bring along the whole auto industry.

According to a Xinhua News Agency report, former Chinese President Jiang Zemin paid his first visit to Volkswagen's headquarters in Wolfsburg, Germany, that year, the first ever by a Chinese official. At that time, Jiang was an official with China's First Machine-building Industry Ministry.

GROWING
W I T H
CHINA
MNC EXECUTIVES
TALK ABOUT CHINA

266

In 1983, the first Santana assembled by Shanghai Volkswagen rolled out of production line.

Jiang reviewed the German auto industry and came up with the idea of introducing Volkswagen technology to China. Volkswagen reacted very positively, saying if China would like to cooperate, Volkswagen would not only transfer the technologies but also provide part of the capital.

After the Chinese delegation returned, Volkswagen sent a team to Shanghai to research the Shanghai Sedan Plant and then started the discussions, which lasted six years.

Fresh out of the "cultural revolution" (1966-1976), there was no integrated legal system to follow in China, especially for business.

Furthermore, although in 1979 the Chinese government started to permit the ownership of private automobiles, in the early 1980s, even owning a bicycle was still a luxury for many people. With an average salary of less than

Construction of
Shanghai Volkswagen
started on October 12,
1984.

50 *yuan* per month, nobody dared to dream of owning
a car.

To test the production cooperation, the two parties
eventually agreed to first assemble 30,000 of Volkswagen's sedans in Anting, on the northwest outskirts of
Shanghai.

After signing a contract in 1982, the first Volkswagen
Santana auto rolled off the assembly line a year later.

In October, 1984, during former German Chancellor
Helmut Kohl's visit to China, the joint venture contract
between Shanghai Automotive Industry Corp and Volkswagen was eventually signed, under a term of 25 years.

"The 50-50 investment measure and most terms in the
Shanghai Volkswagen contract later became the main
items in China's joint venture law and continue to be

used by most ventures today," says Zhang Suixin, executive vice-president of Volkswagen Group China.

"We started everything from scratch. Parts supply chain, qualified staff, related legal systems and many other things in the industry appeared along with the foundation of Shanghai Volkswagen (SVW). China's automotive industry was far below the international average level 30 years ago," recalls Vahland.

However, "the birth of SVW put an end to China's history of making cars behind closed doors at a low technical level and blazed a path of utilizing foreign capital and introducing overseas technology for an accelerated development of the Chinese car making industry", he says.

"While commenting on the past development of Volkswagen in China, external sources have been quoted as calling Volkswagen the company that helped to 'put China on wheels'."

While expanding its production scale, SVW started the Santana endeavor to revitalize the Chinese parts supply industry.

When Santana first came to Shanghai, SVW found that there were no parts plants that could support them in the country, all production lines needed to be reconstructed, thousands of car parts except tires, radios and tape decks, speakers, antennas, and logos, depended on imports, and the localization rate was only 2.7 percent.

Under the circumstances, the entire project could have been defeated by high tariffs and the cost of some accessories.

SVW's drive to get parts made in China also began to clear the way for the entire Chinese auto industry.

They stuck by the principle of the "China Brand" and "no substitutions", and established an institution that regularly met to localize Santana and the domestic supplies rate eventually rose from 2.7 percent to the current 98.9 percent.

SVW's auto parts support network in China now has 400 members in 20 provinces and cities.

SVW is not the only winner. Its actions also established the base for China's car parts industry.

After former German Chancellor Gerhard Schroeder visited Shanghai Volkswagen in November, 1999, he

In November 1991, the contract of Volkswagen's second joint venture in China co-invested with FAW was signed in Beijing.

GROWING
W I T H
CHINA
MNC EXECUTIVES
TALK ABOUT CHINA

270

said, "Shanghai Volkswagen is the successful apotheosis of the Sino-German cooperation."

In 1991, Volkswagen established its second joint venture with First Automotive Works. In December, the first Jetta sedan, Volkswagen's star model, rolled out of the production line in Changchun, Jilin Province.

Four years later, the German automaker made the decision to bring its luxury brand Audi in the joint venture, and in 1996 the first Audi 200 V6 hit the Chinese market.

When Audi's star model A6's came into the market in 1999, the locally-produced sedan with a competitive price soon won the luxury market with sales of record 6,911 units that year.

New Bora, Volkswagen's star model which has been locally produced in FAW-Volkswagen in Changchun, Jilin Province.

Since then, Audi has kept its leading position and was the first luxury sedan brand to break the sales barrier of 100,000 autos in China in 2007, far ahead of its international rivals Mercedes-Benz and BMW.

In 2005, Volkswagen introduced another brand Skoda to Shanghai Volkswagen and in 2007 the made-in-China Skoda Octavia came on the market.

In the first half of 2008, the company sold more than 500,000 cars in China and Vahland says he is confident that the one million mark will be reached by the end of the year.

Olympic Partner

When Vahland took over as president and CEO at Volkswagen Group China in 2005, the company was recording huge losses and was in desperate need of change.

The new CEO knew he needed an idea that would inspire his workforce; and the Olympics came to his mind.

"You always need a good name. Something that people can remember the Olympics is something positive. It's about striving to win," says Vahland.

His idea evolved into the "Olympic Restructure Program", which over the past three years has helped Volkswagen Group China to significantly reduce its costs and boost efficiency by 40 percent by 2008.

GROWING
WITH
CHINA
MNC EXECUTIVES
TALK ABOUT CHINA

272

In 2004, Volkswagen beat its rivals to be the exclusive official automobile partner and supplier of the Beijing 2008 Olympic Games. It was the first Olympic connection for the company.

Volkswagen Group China, together with its Chinese joint ventures, Shanghai Volkswagen and FAW-Volkswagen, supplied a fleet of 959 new vehicles to accompany the Olympic flame on its way across China to Beijing.

It also provided 5,000 vehicles to the Beijing Organizing Committee for the Games of the XXIX Olympiad (BOCOG) for athletes and VIPs, and an Olympic Green Fleet of 30 vehicles "representing Volkswagen's world-leading technology on energy conservation and emission control", says Vahland.

New Audi A6L sedan produced by FAW-Volkswagen in Changchun, Jilin Province.

A green fleet including 30 Volkswagen vehicles equipped with world's leading energy conservation and environmentally friendly technologies runs before Bird's Nest, a major stadium of Beijing 2008 Olympics.

In response to China's 11th Five-Year Plan (2006-2010) which includes goals to reduce energy consumption per unit of GDP by 20 percent and greenhouse gas emission by 10 percent by 2010, in 2007, Volkswagen Group China also began a Powertrain Strategy, in which it promised to reduce the fuel consumption and tailpipe emission of all Volkswagen products in China by 20 percent by 2010 with the TSI engine and DSG gearbox which feature low fuel consumption and high power output.

In addition, Volkswagen and Tongji University have worked on joint research programs including the development of solar hybrid and fuel cell cars and a diesel-powered taxi demonstration project.

"We are aiming to be a high-efficiency, energy-saving and environmentally friendly company. This is Volkswagen China's long-term commitment toward sustainable development," says Vahland.

GROWING
W I T H
CHINA
MNC EXECUTIVES
TALK ABOUT CHINA

274

Winfried Vahland,
President and CEO
of Volkswagen
Group China

Carrying VW's Torch

This is a most memorable year for Winfried Vahland, president and CEO of Volkswagen Group China.

On Aug 6, not only did he run a leg of the Olympic torch relay in Beijing, but he was also lucky enough to pass the flame on to his wife Vahland Ingrid, an act the pair sealed with a kiss.

More important for the CEO was that his company made a new sales record of 531,612 autos in the first half of 2008, a 23.3 percent rise over 2007, which makes Vahland confident about his 2008 target of one million units.

Thanks to his successful Olympic marketing, Volkswagen Group China presented a "big gift" to itself ahead of its 25th birthday in China.

Enjoying living in China with his wife and cherishing his working experience in China, Vahland shares his views with reporter on China's 30 years of development and his company's part in it.

Q: What's the biggest challenge for you and your company in the Chinese market?

A: When I first came to China, my biggest challenge was how to stop our free-fall drop in the market share and regain our position as the market leader.

We launched the "Olympic Restructure Program" in 2005. Three years later, I am very happy and proud to tell people that we've already reached our target successfully.

Thirty years ago, Volkswagen entered China with lots of risks. We needed to build up the groundwork of parts manufacturing in terms of international standards, and also needed to maintain the quality standard of the product. We also needed to reach the target of localization rate on time according to the set schedule.

To reach this target, we set up a parts supply chain and began training staff members to develop skilled and qualified workers. They were trained by retired German experts who were invited to China for a know-how transfer.

Q: What's your comment on your company's development in China and what's China's significance for Volkswagen?

A: China's territory is huge. Every regional market has different features. It's a challenge to automakers from abroad. However, we have two great Chinese partners (SAIC and FAW), who have helped us greatly in adapting with the Chinese market. They have helped us to know Chinese consumers and markets deeply.

We firmly believed China would provide Volkswagen with a unique opportunity in our strategic development. Rooting ourselves in China has proven to be one of our best strategic moves.

Q: As president of a multinational company's China operations, what is your view on China's 30 years of reform and opening?

A: It's a very foresighted policy, which promised China such a bright future. Thirty years ago, China's leaders intelligently opened the country. Reform and opening was the beginning of China's speedy development.

The development of the automotive industry is one of the most rapid among industries. Volkswagen has been very lucky to grow up in China with its two joint ventures.

Q: What's your comment on China's huge changes in the past years?

A: Since my first visit to China in 1993, I have found it so impressive that no matter how often I visit a place in China, there are always lots of changes.

I never have doubts about China's future, since the country is so dynamic and its people are so intelligent and diligent.

By LI FANGFANG

The World Bank
INVESTMENT RETURNS

GROWING
W I T H
CHINA
MNC EXECUTIVES
TALK ABOUT CHINA

278

The year 1980 was not generally considered a water-
shed year in China's history, far less important than
1978, when the country started to experiment with a
new economic regime that would break away from the
old planned economy.

But for the World Bank, 1980 held special significance
— that was when China resumed its representation on
the board of the bank, a move that would have pro-
found bearing on China, the bank and the world.

In the following three decades, the World Bank has
grown rapidly together with China and served as a key
player in the nation's historic growth.

Twenty-eight years on, China has established a solid
market economy and continues to expand its economic
prowess across the spectrum.

Now it has begun to build a more environmentally responsible and energy-efficient economy, goals the World
Bank also puts at the top of its list.

"In the early period, the bank's focus was on the building blocks of the market economy," says David Dollar,
the World Bank's country director for China.

David Dollar,
the World Bank's
country director for
China

Those are principles now well established, but during the early period of China's reform and opening-up,
many people — from policymakers to peasants — were
uncertain whether the country should pursue that path.

Private enterprises and unfettered sales of goods were
still rare and there was significant opposition to the
"residue of capitalism". Such activities even risked jail
before 1978.

The first step for the World Bank was to help the Chinese
people learn what market economy meant and how to go
about it.

"The very first project was to support Chinese universities to improve their technology and help change their
curriculum to make it more relevant (to) the market
economy," Dollar says.

GROWING
W I T H
CHINA
MNC EXECUTIVES
TALK ABOUT CHINA

280

The bank's first project in China in 1981 supported Chinese universities to "strengthen higher education and research" just three years after the nation resumed widespread college enrollment, which had been interrupted by the "cultural revolution" (1966-1976). The effort included fellowships, civil work, equipment, specialist services and other engagement with 26 leading Chinese universities, opening a new chapter in the bank's history.

More major educational support from the bank came in the mid-1990s, when together with the Ford Foundation, it established the China Center for Economic Research at Peking University. Justin Yifu Lin, director of the center, was appointed chief economist and senior vice-president of the bank, marking a milestone in its relationship with China.

The bank also had a hand in China's efforts to establish a national unified grain market, its development of commercial banks and the formulation of an energy approach to charge prices that covered costs of power generation, all crucial to a market economy.

Dollar had not then joined the bank, but had great interest as he chose to study Chinese history and culture in college in the wake of former President Richard Nixon's historic visit to China.

In 1986, Dollar, an economics professor at the University of California, Los Angeles, came to China to teach market economy for six months at the graduate school of the Chinese Academy of Social Sciences, the nation's leading academic institution.

Zhu Guangyao (right), then head of the international department of the Ministry of Finance, shaked hands with David Dollar, the World Bank's country director for China, at a 2006 ceremony to mark the signing of a loan extension agreement. China used the US$20 million in funding to improve governmental functions in its central and western regions, as well as in the country's northeastern industrial belt.

His China tenure prompted him to leave his post as an economics professor and join the World Bank.

The decision "was influenced by my experience in China. It was very interesting and I found it's more interesting to work in the developing countries", he says.

Apart from helping establish a market economy, the World Bank in its early China years made alleviation of poverty one of its primary goals, extending large loans for the campaign. Urban development, infrastructure, healthcare and education were also priorities for the bank.

Dollar became country director for China in 2004 at a time that the bank had already realized the nation had entered a new phase and strategies needed to change.

The population now living in poverty has been reduced to 26 million from 250 million in 1978. China's economy

GROWING
W I T H
CHINA
MNC EXECUTIVES
TALK ABOUT CHINA

282

has become the fourth-largest of the world. For the first time, China contributed more than the US to the annual world economic growth in 2007.

"In the early stage of reform, the World Bank worked with a lot of basic issues in the market economy and China has been very successful," says Dollar. "China is our most successful partnership."

The World Bank has an independent panel that evaluates its projects, reporting not to management but directly to shareholders, and it "found that more than 90 of our China projects were successful", he says.

The World Bank stopped offering preferential loans in 2000 and now all its funding comes on standard terms. In the past 27 years, the bank has loaned a total of US$42.17 billion to support various Chinese projects.

"China no longer needs a large amount of foreign capital since it has a lot of reserves," says Dollar.

In 2007 the nation became a contributor to the International Development Association (IDA) for the first time, although the amount was not large.

Dollar revealed the contribution could be about US$30 million, a similar amount China donated to the Asian Development Fund in 2004.

"It's reasonable to think the contribution is going to be similar to that kind of funding."

"The amount of the contribution is not that important," Dollar says. "What's important is that China for the first time contributed to IDA. It's a very important milestone."

Environmental Drive

As China's economy steams ahead, the World Bank has shifted its strategy from development to the environment and energy efficiency, two fields in which it has rich experience and where China is finding its way.

The country has drafted targets to cut energy use by 20 percent and emissions by 10 percent by 2010. The bank's support can help the country realize its ambitious plans.

"What's happened in the past couple of years is that the environment has emerging as our main focus (in China)," says Dollar.

Seventy-five percent of the bank's projects in the past three years have direct environmental objectives, he adds.

"Most of the projects focused on cleaning up water pollution, reducing air pollution and increasing energy efficiency."

Reaching Further

The bank has now increased staff numbers in its Beijing office to meet the challenge.

GROWING
W I T H
CHINA
MNC EXECUTIVES
TALK ABOUT CHINA

284

When it first opened an office in Beijing in the 1980s, there were very few staff members and almost all technical expertise was based in Washington, Dollar says. "It was a little bit distant."

About 80 percent of the professional team was from the US, but now it is close to 50 percent, facilitating face-to-face contact with local governments, he notes.

The bank is also considering reaching further afield by establishing more local branch offices in places where it has a number of key projects.

In Chongqing municipality, for example, the World Bank president Robert Zoellick discussed the issue with the municipality head Bo Xilai during his December visit to China.

"We are seriously exploring it," Dollar says.

The World Bank is now keen to spread China's successful experience to other developing countries, such as those on the African continent.

"We can develop a training course that is focused on the lessons from China," says Dollar. "There's so much interest (from Africa)."

Dollar also suggests that developing countries should have more communication to share their development experiences.

By XIN ZHIMING

On a Song

When Deng Xiaoping convinced the nation 30 years ago that a new direction in development with greater openness and reliance on market mechanisms was needed, China was a small factor in the global economy. Today it is a key trading partner of many countries around the world and one of the key drivers of global growth.

In fact, it is at the center of what future historians may call the greatest economic transformation the world has ever seen. International trade flows, capital markets and even development assistance programs are changing dramatically as a result of China's growth and successful economic transformation. Once the largest recipient of the World Bank assistance, China has become a donor to the International Development Association and recently formed a partnership with the World Bank to provide development assistance to Africa.

So far the economic reforms and opening-up that were started 30 years ago have yielded great benefits for China and for the rest of the world. What will the next 30 years bring? Will the existing superpower resist the emergence of a multi-polar world? Or will wiser heads prevail and collaborate to ensure that the world, including the poor, can continue to benefit from rule-based globalization?

Economic statistics and models describe the enormous changes that have taken place in China and its role in the world only very partially and imperfectly. Economists often forget that the essence of development lies in its human, social and cultural dimensions, which are hard to quantify. Allow me to use an example from the world of music to explain what I mean.

While preparing for my assignment as chief of the World Bank's resident mission in China (1993-1997), I learned about the visit of Isaac Stern, the violinist, to Beijing and Shanghai in June 1979, only six months after the historical Third Plenum of the 11th Central Committee which started the opening-up process. Stern was one of the first major Western musicians invited to perform and teach master classes in China after Mao's death. He was impressed by the level of technical proficiency he encountered in music conservatories in both cities, but disappointed at the low level of understanding of Western classical music and the poor quality of musical instruments that were used.

In Beijing Stern found only one piano of sufficient quality for his performance in a violin-piano sonata. In Shanghai he could not find one single high-quality piano. He wanted to ask for the one from Beijing to be brought over to Shanghai, but was afraid that such a request would embarrass his hosts.

Contrast Stern's experience in 1979 with the music scene in China today. In September 2007, while visiting Beijing for economic research, I attended a concert in the Poly Plaza, one of many excellent concert halls in China today, featuring Lang Lang as soloist in Beethoven's second piano concerto. He was accompanied by the Berlin Staatskapelle, one of Germany's finest orchestras, which was conducted by Daniel Barenboim. It was a magnificent performance — it brought tears to my eyes. The audience loved it and couldn't stop applauding.

After the concert I went to a reception that was also attended by Deng Rong, Deng Xiaoping's youngest daughter, co-founder and chairwoman of the Beijing International Music Festival which celebrated its 10th anniversary. The symbolism of the events that evening was striking. China's miracle is certainly not limited to the economic arena. The country has reached out and opened up in many areas of human, social and cultural development. The Olympics in Beijing in 2008 has showcased this globally.

Opening-up is not only good for business, it also serves cultural development.

Now that the most critical economic reforms have essentially been completed, the question that naturally arises is: will the Party be as successful in transforming the political system as it has been in transforming the economy?

The challenges facing China today are no less daunting than they were 30 years ago, but they are different in nature. The way in which they are tackled will have enormous domestic and international consequences. China is now facing what might be called the challenge of a second transition: transition to rule of law, social fairness and reduced inequality, transparency and accountability of government, and better protection of the environment. If I am allowed one suggestion in this context it would be to strengthen fiscal programs and policies in support of China's social and environmental objectives.

China's successful pursuit of development through incremental market reforms and openness to foreign trade, investment and ideas, has become a source of inspiration for developing countries in other parts of the world. It has also changed my own thinking about what is important for development. Investment capital, of course, will always be important, but what is even more critical is what money cannot buy: vision, courage and good leadership supported by competent and honest government responsive to the needs of the people.

(Pieter Bottelier, the author of this article, is an international economist, China scholar and consultant. He taught as an adjunct lecturer at Harvard

GROWING
W I T H
CHINA
MNC EXECUTIVES
TALK ABOUT CHINA

288

University's Kennedy School of Government, and as an adjunct professor at Georgetown University's School of Foreign Service. Dr. Bottelier has been an adjunct professor at Johns Hopkins University School of Advanced International Studies since 1999 and was recently named associate professor. He worked at the World Bank between 1970-1998, serving as senior advisor to the vice-president for East Asia, 1997-1998, and was chief of the World Bank's resident mission in Beijing, 1993-1997. The views expressed are his own.)

图书在版编目（CIP）数据

赢之道：跨国公司高管谈改革开放：英文／朱灵主编．
北京：新世界出版社，2008.11
（中外文化交流系列）
ISBN 978-7-80228-992-5
I. 赢… II. 朱… III. 改革开放 – 成就 – 中国 – 英文　IV. D61

中国版本图书馆 CIP 数据核字（2008）第 177027 号

Growing with China: MNC Executives Talk About China
赢之道：跨国公司高管谈改革开放（英文版）

主　　编：朱　灵
策　　划：李淑娟　刘伟玲
编　　委：黄　庆　王西民　曲莹璞　任　侃　刘伟玲　张晓刚　李卫涛
　　　　　吴允和　丁学梅　徐大山　梁宏福
执行编辑：李卫涛　刘伟玲
主要作者：李方方　李卫涛　宛志弘　刘　洁　辛志明　姜　薇　王　星　丁清芬　陆浩婷
　　　　　刁　莹　鲍婉娴　张　冉　庹燕南　王　兰　童　浩　张　琦　傅　瑜
责任编辑：李淑娟　葛文聪
英文审定：徐明强
封面设计：黎　红
装帧设计：黎　红
责任印制：李一鸣　黄厚清
出版发行：新世界出版社
社　　址：北京市西城区百万庄大街24号（100037）
总编室电话：+ 86 10 6899 5424　　68326679（传真）
发行部电话：+ 86 10 6899 5968　　68998705（传真）
本社中文网址：http://www.nwp.cn
本社英文网址：http://www.newworld-press.com
版权部电子信箱：frank@nwp.com.cn
版权部电话：+ 86 10 6899 6306
印　　刷：北京外文印刷厂
经　　销：新华书店
开　　本：787×1092　　1/16
字　　数：180千字　　印张：18.75
版　　次：2009年1月第1版　　2009年1月北京第1次印刷
书　　号：ISBN 978-7-80228-992-5
定　　价：78.00元